D1039833

GLORY IN
MONGOLIA

GLORY IN MONGOLIA

Rick Leatherwood

WILLIAM CAREY
LIBRARY

Scripture taken from the NEW AMERICAN STANDARD BIBLE®,
Copyright © 1960,1962,1963,1968,1971,1972,1973,1975,1977,1995
by The Lockman Foundation. Used by permission.

Cover design and typesetting: Amanda Valloza

Published by William Carey Library
1605 East Elizabeth Street, Pasadena, California 91104
www.WCLBooks.com

William Carey Library is a ministry of the US Center for World Mission,
Pasadena, California

Library of Congress Cataloguing in Publication Data

Leatherwood, Rick.
        Glory in Mongolia/ Rick Leatherwood.
                p. cm.
        ISBN 0-87808-368-5 (alk. paper)
        1. Mongoliwa -- Church history. 2. Inner Mongolia (China) --
        Church history. I. Title.

BR1338.L43 2006
275.1'70829--dc22
2006005810

Printed in the United States of America

Contents

118005

Pictures & Documents

Foreword

Books on pioneer missions are seldom the most popular or among the bestsellers at Barnes & Noble or Waldenbooks today. Pioneer missions is a rather specific category in which the world is not interested. Its stories tell of people who, like Abraham, lived by faith, sometimes lived in tents as did the author of this book, while looking for the city which has foundations, whose architect and builder is God.

Rick Leatherwood is a unique person. Always earnest. Always honest. Always probing for understanding. Assuming nothing and being unassuming, his splendidly intelligent but genuinely humble account of the opening of Mongolia to the gospel is part of the great continuum of the increase of God's kingdom.

Rick has had many tours of duty, which include time in the Philippines with the Maguindanao people, in northern Iraq among the Kurds, and working throughout the 10/40 window to promote the use of the book of Proverbs as a positive, non-threatening point of contact with Muslim peoples. However, his pioneer work in Mongolia ranks very high, and it should. Rick's taking Navajo pastors to Mongolia and exploring the cultural connections between Native Americans and Mongols as a means to share the gospel was inspired, and its success has been talked about in mission classes at seminaries and Bible schools around the world.

This personal account, in clean, clear prose, is often stranger than fiction could ever be. It challenges conventional ideas of what a missionary is and does. The amazing time of the last decade of the twentieth century, in which Rick describes the birth of the church in Mongolia can never happen again, and won't need to. He, his family, and many other intrepid people have now laid the permanent foundation of Jesus Christ, a foundation of marvelous intricacy as you will see. This is a story of high adventure and great significance.

Ralph D. Winter
General Director,
Frontier Mission Fellowship

Preface

Having a book published is a little like living in Jesus' parable of Luke 7:32 that says, "We played the flute for you, and you did not dance; we sang a dirge and you did not cry." Some publishers wanted this, while others wanted that. In the end I am quite pleased to have William Carey Library publish *Glory in Mongolia* and to move beyond the marketplace of flutes and dirges to the amazing reality of the expansion of God's kingdom.

In some ways, *Glory in Mongolia* is like one of the memorial stones Joshua ordered removed from the Jordan. May this book help the Mongols to look back and see the remarkable way that God began to reach out and call them to Himself. In other ways, this book was written to further the unchanging purpose of God in reaching every tribe and tongue and nation in the world with the gospel.

When I first became a missionary, the number of unreached people groups in the world was estimated to be over 16,000. In the course of the last twenty-five years, through the efforts of missionaries and churches around the world, the number of unreached ethnic groups has been reduced to somewhere around 3,000, and the groups who are yet unengaged whose populations exceed 100,000, **is less than 640.*** What these remarkable numbers reveal is the wonderful news that we are clearly moving towards the completion of the Great Commission! It is a wonderful time to be alive and a coworker of Jesus.

The reader should understand that the story told in these pages is my own. The narrative is representative of what God did and is doing,

---

*IMB Finishing the Task Conference, November 2005

but not comprehensive. Many people and organizations not mentioned by name in this book made significant contributions in opening Mongolia. Certainly other Americans, along with the German and Korean missionaries, played major roles in building up the church, as well as others from different lands who gave themselves sacrificially to the Lord in bringing about the movement. To try to list them all and tell their stories would be a task too great and beyond my ability.

It has been a pleasure to know Brian and Louise Hogan over the years as we first met on the Navajo Indian Reservation in 1987. They later served with our mission in Mongolia and now sit on our board of directors. It is friends like the Hogans who make going through the thick and thin of missions a treasure. I am thankful to Brian for his help in editing the manuscript. I also want to thank Ann Steffora Mutchler for further editing and offering her professional expertise. Nancy Narbut and Bekah Mintz did the final proofreading and Amanda Valloza did the typesetting. Thank you all.

And lastly I am grateful to Dr. Ralph Winter for writing the foreword to this book. He is easily the most extraordinary person I have ever met and though the secular history books will never mention his name, like the hidden yeast in the Lord's parable of the kingdom, he has perhaps influenced the world in the last quarter of the twentieth century more than any other man, through his research and founding of the United States Center for World Mission. His impact on my life and countless others has been profound and greatly appreciated over the years.

Rick Leatherwood
Iraq, October, 2006

This book is dedicated to my mother,

who told me when I was young

that if I wasn't good

I would be sent to Outer Mongolia.

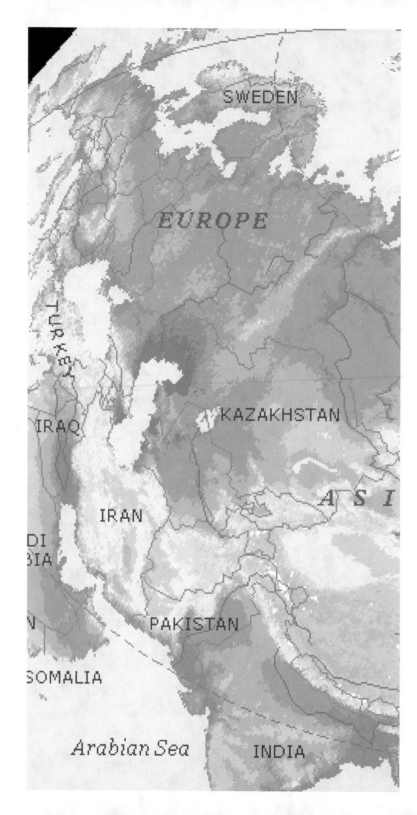

ARCTIC OCEAN

RUSSIA
Arctic Circle

A

MONGOLIA

CHINA

Tropic of Cancer

Introduction

In the course of history, empires have been built by the likes of Ramses, Nebuchadnezzar, Alexander, Caesar, Napoleon, and Genghis Khan. They came, they conquered, they constructed their palaces, took their bows, were placed in their tombs, and exited the world stage. Yet in the very midst of these kingdoms, often imperceptibly, another kingdom was at work– the kingdom of God, growing, expanding, and extending itself throughout the earth, not unlike leaven permeating a loaf of bread. It does not come to destroy or rule by force. It comes quietly, unobtrusively, secretly, working in the hearts of men and women through persuasion rather than power[1], bringing forth the truth that of the increase of God's kingdom there will be no end.

The increase of that kingdom made its way to the borders of Mongolia on three occasions. The first occurred in the era of the Great Khans when the news of Jesus Christ was royally welcomed by the court of the Khans. However, though the emissaries of Christ brought the good news to the court of the Khan, they failed to bring it to the common man. Consequently though history records some believers among the Mongols in the thirteenth century, there is no mention of the church having been established there at that time, and so knowledge of Christ disappeared when the empire collapsed.

The second time the gospel came to the Mongols was in the late nineteenth and early twentieth centuries. This attempt, though noble and inspired, unfortunately saw little success. Though the messengers were

---

1 Eldon Ladd, *The Gospel of the Kingdom*, Eerdmans

fervent and faithful, giving up their lives and blood, again no church took root and it seemed the gospel would have to wait for another day to flourish in Mongolia.

This is the story of the third time the news that a man has risen from the dead came to the Mongol people and of the birth of the church in that nation. When Christ came to the earth, he said, "You shall know the truth, and the truth shall set you free." Like the eternity that has been put in the heart of man to know the truth, the desire to be free has also been placed in people by God. Like truth, freedom is part of his image in which man was created.

The satisfaction that comes from people being free to exercise their own political authority brings a certain kind of contentment. They are, to some degree, in control of their own lives and destiny. However this blessing was denied the Mongolian people for over six hundred years. For in the period of time extending from the fourteenth to the twentieth century, the Mongols were forced to live under the authority of the Chinese, and then that of the Soviet Union.

And so with the desire for freedom yearning in their hearts, it didn't take long for the revolution that brought down the Berlin wall in the fall of 1989, to be embraced by the Mongol people as well. They too wanted to be free. And so the young leaders of the democratic movement in Mongolia fasted before the nation, and then called for the Communist government to step down. Their young leader Zorig, whose name literally means courage and who was one of the few Mongols at that time who had heard of Christ and knew something of the ways of God, with wisdom in his heart, urged the huge crowd that had swelled to more than 100,000 people to remain peaceful.

The tension built as more and more people came into the city square. The Mongol people wondered what the men in the parliament building at the end of the square were thinking as they looked down from their lofty windows at the growing multitude. And more importantly, what would those leaders do? Who were they? Were they really Communists, or were they still Mongols in their hearts?

Suddenly the doors opened and a government official stepped forward with papers in hand. The crowd of a hundred thousand Mongols quieted down as their young leader Zorig called for attention and handed the bullhorn to the government official who then read the announcement. The Communist leaders had resigned, and the Parliament was calling for democratic elections to be held as soon as possible. The crowd roared. The Mongols were free again. People cheered and clasped each other's arms. They sang, they danced, they wept. They were free. It was Sunday, March 11, 1990.

For the preceding seven decades the Mongols had known little about what had gone on in the rest of the world, and the rest of the world knew very little about them. In 1921, Mongolia had been forced to become the second Communist country in the world, and as the iron hand of Soviet Communism consolidated its hold on Mongolia, communications with the outside world were severed, and virtually all information was thereafter filtered through Moscow. Mongolia was closed.

The Mongol people were cut off from the world and for the next seventy years they would live in isolation with few visitors from the West allowed in. The Mongols accepted Communism, some willingly, others by force, and Mongolia became a social welfare state of the Soviet Union. Their literature and art would take on the form and terminology of the party. Their stories would begin to revolve around the greatness of the Communist system.

Though not a lot was known about Mongolia in 1990 by people in the West, there was some vague recollection of a conqueror named Genghis Khan. However, though the name of Genghis Khan was familiar to the West, the character of the Mongol people and their history were not known. Who were these people whom the world had heard about, but knew so little? What was their real story?

CHAPTER 1

The Mongol Khans Hear of the Christ

"And the Lord scattered them abroad
over the face of the whole earth."
Genesis 11:9

The Mongols, as they call themselves, have roamed the grasslands of central Asia for all of recorded history. Just how long they were there before that, no one really knows. They are credited with the rather significant invention of the stirrup. They were a nomadic people, who followed their herds of sheep and goats, yaks, cows, and camels, and of course their beloved horses, and had little care for the rest of the world.

But there was one notable exception. This was a young man named Temujin, born in AD 1164 who gathered his brothers together and set out to avenge his father's death, which had come by treachery at the hands of a neighboring clan. Through the valor of Temujin, victory was realized, and the two tribes became one. So began the uniting of the Mongol people. From there, other clans were subdued, and by 1206, the scattered tribes of peoples living on the grasslands called the steppe had become a nation and Temujin was given the title of Genghis Khan, meaning Genghis the king. This Mongol wanted to conquer the world.

The Secret History of the Mongols, written in 1242, gives an enlightening look into the Mongol culture of the thirteenth century. Though *The History* begins by saying, "There was a bluish wolf which was born having its destiny from Heaven above," Genghis Khan was certainly no myth. Young Temujin, who became Genghis, was real, and seldom has the world seen one so ruthless, conquering cities and cultures far superior to his own. How could this have happened? The answer is actually quite straightforward. In the thirteenth century, the world had simply come to a point in its history where it was ripe to be conquered by a horse culture, and the Mongols were the epitome of a horse culture. In an era when most people on the earth traveled a distance of five to fifteen miles in a day, the Mongol army could ride 120, 150, or even 180 miles in a single twenty-four hour period. For alongside the army of 100,000 horsemen, galloped a *ramada* of 800,000 horses, supplying fresh mounts throughout the day for the Khan's army. When the Mongol army was on the march, it is said they would sometimes prick a vein in their horse's neck and drink the blood so as not to have to stop to prepare meals, and thus be able to keep on the move. And the Mongols moved swiftly, literally taking the world by surprise, and by storm, and as they kept moving and conquering, the Mongol Empire eventually came to be the largest the world has ever known. At its height it stretched from the South China Sea of the Pacific, to the Danube River in Europe.

In reading *The Secret History*, one catches a glimpse of a unique people who lived close to the land and were filled with passion. They seem to be a rare mixture of the melancholic and the choleric. Poetry is laced throughout *The Secret History* and music... ah, music! Music was born in Mongolia, or so the Mongols say. How could this aggressiveness that is so clearly evident in the Mongols be joined together with such a laconic nature in one nation of human beings? On the day Temujin met his bride, his future father-in-law said to his father;

> "This thy son is a son with fire in his eyes and light in his face."
> Then of his own clan he said,
> "Having for us the comeliness of the daughters of our daughters, and the beauty of our daughters, we do not dispute empire.

For those of you which are become Khan,
we make our daughters comely of cheek to ride in a cart with wheels,
And making one to harness a black he camel to it, making
him to trot, we go unto the Khan,
And make them to sit at one of the sides of the Khan on a high throne.
As for our boys, regard our encampment (wealth of animals),
As for our girls, their beauty is beheld."

But alongside this melancholic temperament, hot blood ran through the Mongol's veins, and for a taste of it, listen to the words of Temujin's mother, also recorded in *The Secret History,* scathing at him and his brothers upon learning they had killed a man.

"A lash in the eye; an impediment in the mouth.
You have no companion other than your shadow;
You have no whip other than a tail.
When he fiercely issued forth from my hot womb,
This one (Temujin) was born holding a black clot of blood in his hand.
Even as the Qasar dog, which eats its own afterbirth;
Even as the panther which rushes at the cliff;
Even as the lion which is not able to repress his fury;
Even as the python which says, 'I will swallow my prey alive.'
Even as the gerfalcon which rushes at his own shadow;
Even as the curaca fish which swallows in silence;
Even as the camel which bites the heel of his colt;
Even as the wolf, which relies upon the snow storm to stalk his prey;
Even as the mandarin duck which because it is not able to overtake his chickens, eats his chicks;
Even as the jackal, which if one touch him, makes a league with others to defend his den;
Even as the tiger, which in seizing his prey doth not hesitate;
Even as the bear, which rushes foolishly upon his prey, You have destroyed!
At the moment when you have no companion other than your shadow;
At the moment when you have no whip other than a tail.
Citing ancient words;
Quoting old words;
she was exceedingly displeased with her sons.

Loyalty to the Khan came to be the highest of virtues for the Mongols, which is seen throughout *The Secret History*. On the day he was made Khan, Genghis said,

> Being named by powerful Heaven,
> Effecting this by Mother Earth
> The male has taken his vengeance.
> And as for the Merkid people,
> We have made their breasts to become empty,
> And we have broken off a piece of their liver.
> We have made their beds to become empty,
> And we have made an end of the men of their descendants.
> And we have ravished those of the women which remained.

As becomes evident in reading *The Secret History*, vengeance is just as dominant a theme as loyalty.

> Till the nails of your five fingers disappear through wear;
> Till your ten fingers are worn away through rubbing, strive to avenge me.
> To avenge the avengement, to requite the requital.[2]

Up until the time of Genghis Khan, the rest of the world had never heard of Mongolia. But while England was formulating its Magna Carta (1215), and the Byzantine Empire was enjoying prosperity throughout Persia, Genghis Khan was honing his military skills in China and welding the Mongols into the most formidable war machine the world had ever known. As a result, the knights of Europe in their three hundred pounds of armor were no match for the fleet Mongol warriors who could ride circles around their European adversaries, and were deft shots with their bows.

Great cities in central Asia like Bukhara and Samar Khan, were grand and formidable cities, but their bellies were soft, and their intelligence reports lacking, and before they knew it, Genghis Khan had their cities by the throat and began pounding them with machinery of war he had learned during his

---

2 Francis Cleaves, translator & editor, *The Secret History of the Mongols*, (Cambridge, Massachusetts: Harvard, 1982) p. 23

conquest of the Chinese. These Persians were gentle, domestic people living in cities. The Mongols lived in tents, and what is more, were still a people who lived totally off the land. Conquering China, Persia, Russia, and Eastern Europe was something like a wolf attacking a dog. It was no contest. Only the death of Ogedi Khan in 1241, who had taken over after the death of his father Genghis in 1227, halted the Mongol conquest of Europe, as the armies retreated to their homeland to await the selection of a new Khan.

The Russians seemed to have suffered the greatest psychological damage by the Mongols, not knowing just what to do with these unknown, uncivilized, aliens who simply appeared out of nowhere. Who were they? Where had they come from? Why were they destroying everything in sight? To Russians, the rule of The Golden Horde was the greatest nightmare of their history. The domination by the Mongols in Russia would last some two hundred and fifty years until AD 1480, and is widely documented, so its details will not be gone into here.

After first attacking and conquering China, by 1231 the Mongol armies under Genghis Khan's son, Ogedi, overran what is modern day Iran, Mesopotamia, Armenia, and Georgia. In 1258 Baghdad, the seat of the Abbasid caliphate, was captured. The Persian Khanate was established by Hulagu, grandson of Genghis and brother to Kublai. Hulagu styled himself Il-Khan (the king) and ruled over what is today Iran, eastern Iraq, western Afghanistan, and Turkmenistan. The Khans of Iran eventually accepted the faith of Islam.

But going back to Genghis Khan, after uniting the Mongol tribes in 1206, the first non-Mongol people whom Genghis would conquer were called the Kerait. Two hundred years earlier, the Kerait people had become Christians when the king of the Kerait became lost in a blizzard, the trying ordeal of which then lead to his conversion. His amazing story was then related in a letter addressed to the bishop of Baghdad in 1020, from the bishop of Merv, in Turkmenistan, whose name was Ebedjesus. Here we have a piece of his story:

The King of the *Kerait* people... while he was hunting... and having got into the snow and lost his way, suddenly saw a saint, who thus addressed him, 'If you will believe in Christ, I will show you a way on which you shall not perish.' Then did the king promise to become a sheep in Christ's fold. Having been shown the way, the king on reaching home summoned the Christian merchants (Nestorians from the Syrian church) who were at his court and adopted their faith. Having received a copy of the gospels, which he read daily, he sent me a messenger with the request that I should go to him, or send him a priest who should baptise him. [3]

And so it was, that after Genghis Khan conquered the Kerait, being an astute politician as well as a military genius, he married off a number of his sons to Keriat princesses. As a result, in the years of the great Khans of the mid-thirteenth century, though it is overlooked in most histories, Christians held high offices in the court of the Khans. One of these princesses would become the mother of Kublai Khan.

Being raised by a Christian mother, it was Kublai Khan that Marco Polo's father, Niccolò, met in 1267. It appears Niccolò was well received by Kublai Khan, and he must have witnessed to him about the Christ, for he was sent back to Italy with a command that one hundred Christian teachers be sent to the Mongolian court to instruct Kublai Khan and his people in the ways of Jesus Christ. Here is the edict:

> To send 100 persons well skilled in your law, who being confronted with the idolaters (ie Buddhists) shall have power to coerce them, and showing that they themselves are endowed with similar art... When I am witness of this, I shall place them and their religion under an interdict, and allow myself to be baptised. Following my example, all my nobility will then in like manner receive baptism, and this will be imitated by my subjects in general; so that the Christians of these parts shall exceed in number those who inhabit your own country.[4]

---

3   Hugh Kemp, *Steppe by Step.* Kemp is quoting: H.H.Horworth, *History of the Mongols*, 9th-19th Centuries, London: Burt and Franklin, 1876
4   Hugh Kemp, *Marco Polo: The Travels of Marco Polo*, E. Rhys (translator) London: J.M.Dent & Sons Ltd. 1908.

Kublai Khan

But when Niccolò returned to Italy with the invitation from Kublai Khan, the reigning Pope had just died and it was two years before a successor, Pope Gregory, was selected to the papacy. He responded to Kublai Khan's invitation by sending only two monks, who did set out towards Mongolia, but upon reaching the shores of Turkey, evidently being the unadventurous sort and preferring the comforts of home to the rigors of the road, they turned back. And that is the unfortunate story of what has become known as, 'The greatest missed opportunity in the history of Christian missions.'

John of Montecorvino arrived in the capitol of Cambuluc in 1294, which later was to be known as Peking, and is now Beijing. Though Kublai Khan had just died, Montecorvino was well received by the court, though this was probably comprised more of sedentary Chinese than of Mongols, as most Mongols still lived their nomadic lifestyle up on the steppe beyond the Gobi Desert. Montecorvino preached, won converts, built a church, and even translated the New Testament, though probably into Chinese as the Mongols had no written language at the time. Even *The Secret History of the Mongols*, published in 1242, was originally written in Chinese and only later translated into Mongolian.

In Chinese history, the period of Mongol rule is simply referred to as the Yuan dynasty. While in China, you will never hear about the period when the Mongols ruled, unless you specifically ask. Apparently this is not a part of their history that the Chinese like to look back upon. Furthermore, from having been conquered and ruled by the Mongols, the succeeding Ming emperor became exceedingly xenophobic, and over-reacted to the extreme, burning all books of a foreign nature such as the Scriptures that had been translated by John of Montecorvino. Consequently, two hundred years later, in the mid-sixteenth century, when the devout Catholic priest Niccolò Ricci arrived in Cambuluc (Peking) with his wonderful clocks, he found no trace of Christianity.

After the Mongol empire collapsed in 1368, under the sheer weight of its enormity, with no other Mongols apparently possessing the military genius of Genghis or administrative genius of Kublai Khan, the emperor of the Ming dynasty cleverly brought Tibetan Buddhism into Mongolia to pacify the warlike spirit of the Mongols. In this he preceded Marx's understanding of religion as "the opiate of the people" by some five hundred years. The emperor's strategy was most effective, and the Mongols disappeared from the world stage. It would be half a millennium before they were once again contacted with the good news that a man had risen from the dead.

James Gilmore has often been acclaimed as the apostle to the Mongols. He came to Mongolia in 1872, from Scotland, having been sent out by the London Missionary Society, and arrived in Mongolia after traveling overland through Russia. By any missionary standard, James Gilmore proceeded to do just about everything right. He lived with the people, as one of the people. He ate their food, learned their language, wore their clothes, froze when they froze, and went hungry when the people were hungry. And yet as he lay dying in Mongolia some twenty-one years later, having never taken a furlough, Gilmore said he could count his converts on one hand, and none had been baptized. It seemed that Buddhism had such a hold on the Mongols at this time that the message that Gilmore preached could not get through. But perhaps in God's economy, today's harvest is reaped from what this man and others sowed with their lives.

The next missionaries to Mongolia were from Sweden and they too met with the same spiritual resistance and indifference to the message of the gospel as had Gilmore. Many of these Swedish missionaries paid the supreme price and were martyred during the Boxer rebellion.

Ironically, at the dawn of the twentieth century, Mongolia was possibly the most religious country in the world! The Buddhism that had been introduced five centuries earlier had taken root, and over the course of the next five centuries, its religious practices became ingrained in the Mongols like the hair on their horses' backs. And as the eldest son of every family was given to the local monastery to be trained as a lama, we have a country that gave away the strength of its first born to foster its religion.

China dominated Mongolia for those five hundred years, creating inevitable resentment. However as the Mongols, like all other peoples, have been created in the image of God, they longed to be free. There was an uprising in 1911 when the Mongols broke loose for a while, but the Chinese quickly regained control until 1921. Then the young Mongol leader Sukhebaatar asked for the help of the Russian government. The help was granted, but it came with an unspoken price that had a rather strong string attached. Sukhebaatar and the Mongols certainly did not want to be Communists. They wanted to be free. With the help of the Russians, the Chinese were forced out of Mongolia. But the attached string was soon pulled, and when Sukhebaatar balked at the orders coming down from Moscow in 1924, he was invited to Russia for a visit. There, in Moscow, it seems this young, vibrant, thirty year-old Sukhebaatar, who was a keen shot with a bow from the back of a galloping horse, became ill after dinner one night, and the flower of the Mongolian nation was laid to rest. With that, the Mongols moved from bad to worse, and into the fire of the Soviets, and a paranoid madman named Stalin.

In the 1930s, the Communists murdered the hapless unarmed monks by the tens of thousands! Monasteries from one end of Mongolia to the other were razed to the ground, as the country became a bloodbath.

Even these many years later, at the beginning of the twenty-first century, there are those in Mongolia who still remember the night when their father or grandfather disappeared into the night, never to be heard of again, as the *Commintern* eliminated anyone who had an education, or was simply suspect by the government.

So whether they liked it or not, the Mongols became good comrades, which is just what the leaders in the Kremlin wanted. After World War II, what the Soviets desired was that the Mongols would become something of a human buffer between themselves and the Chinese. And so 80,000 Russian troops were stationed in Mongolia, the majority of them down near the Chinese border. Then to keep the peace and the semblance of autonomy, the Mongols were allowed to form a kind of shadow government within their own borders, but of course there were Soviet advisors at every level. What was the price to Russia of this human shield? Merely a few bushels of wheat, for along with the not too subtle reality of their guns, it is now clear that the Russians had bought the Mongols for a bottle of vodka. To the Russians, this was simply inexpensive wheat of which they had plenty. But for the Mongols, the social and spiritual costs kept growing over time, for which they are still paying heavily.

But to be fair, the Soviets also brought the Mongols into the twentieth century. In 1921, Mongolia had no hospitals, no banks, and no public schools. There were no houses apart from that of the head lama's, and no buildings other than the monasteries. The people were almost totally illiterate, except for the lamas, some of whom had learned to read Tibetan. Mongolia was an extremely backward nation. But then to a degree, and for a price, the Russians helped bring them forward. Schools, a health care system, and some basic transportation and communication infrastructures were established. Over time the literacy rate rose to a high level. Today some Mongols are appreciative for these things, especially those who received the spoils of the system, while others remain bitter over the insanity of the purges under Stalin, and at having been essentially colonized for seventy years.

However, along with the slogans and doctrines of Communism that were taught in schools and plastered on every wall that afforded itself, also came the erosion of religion and the grip that Satan had upon these people through Buddhism. The result was that when the curtain opened, and it was possible for people from the free world to enter Mongolia again, it was apparent that a spiritual vacuum had been created.

CHAPTER 2

Jesus Christ? Who is Jesus Christ?

"I have other sheep that are not of this fold. I must bring them also.
They too will listen to my voice, and there shall be one flock."
John 10:16

It is hard to imagine a whole nation of people near the close of the twentieth century, with cars and buses, schools and hospitals, hotels and hot running water, along with their horses, cows, sheep, goats, and camels, a country with membership in the United Nations and which took part in the Olympic games, whose people had virtually no knowledge that a man named Jesus had ever walked on the earth. But the fact is that as late as 1990, the Mongols as a people had little to no knowledge of Christ.

Very few people from the West had ever been to Mongolia. Technically they were their own country, but in reality the Mongols were part of the Soviet Union. They knew of the achievements that had been made by the Soviets, and even had one of their own Mongol people who had flown in outer space as a cosmonaut. But except for how they fit into the plans of the Soviet Union, their thinking was mostly provincial. And to the rest of the world, Mongolia was a mystery.

"Why have you come to our country?" asked the Mongolian government official, looking in wonder at the Navajo Indian standing in front of him.

"You see, the story of my people is that long ago we came across the Bering Straight from Mongolia, and I wanted to come over here and find out more about this." replied Milt Shirleson, the Navajo.

To this, the Mongol looked at Milt and said in a most curious way, "We have the same story in our history, that long ago a group of our people broke off and started walking east across the Bering Straight and are today the American Indians."

A year earlier the Lord had given me a vision for taking Native American Christians to Mongolia, believing that the cultural similarities between the two would act like a bridge from which we could share the gospel. The government official was named Ganbold, director of the Mongolian Peace and Friendship Society. He was tall and articulate, a good looking man from a prominent family who had been well educated in Moscow. Except for our guide, he was the only Mongol we had met up until then who spoke English. His office was lined with hundreds of books and he himself was obviously well read. Ganbold ordered tea, and a few minutes later a young woman entered the room carrying a tray with tea and sweets. The Mongols are well known for their hospitality and graciousness, and Ganbold was highly skilled in the art of protocol, paying great attention to detail.

He had talked of history and culture, leading him to ask Milt Shirleson about his reasons for coming to Mongolia. It was obvious that he was genuinely interested in this apparent ancient relative, a Native American who had returned to Mongolia. The dynamic of their relationship was extraordinary to watch.

They explored language, and found a few common words such as 'snow,' and 'where,' which were the same. Also intriguing was the fact that the shape and size of the round Mongolian tent called a ger, and the eight-sided Navajo hogan, are almost identical, though the Navajo living in the warmth of Arizona, point their door to the rising sun of the east, whereas the Mongols point their door to the south, away from the blisteringly cold wind from the north.

Ganbold and Milt Shirleson

The fact that both the Mongols and the Native Americans looked alike and had identical stories was fascinating, but were the Mongols and Native Americans really related? Had there been a migration across a land bridge that is now called the Bering Straight? Can it truly be said that Native Americans came from the Mongols, and that they were once the same people? There is certainly great similarity in their physical appearance, but this would not necessarily confirm the link. The conversation went on and on, and finally the Navajo, Milt Shirleson, looked at Ganbold and asked, "Do your babies have a little bluish spot in the small of their back when they are born?" Ganbold smiled at Milt and replied, "Yes they do." Milt returned the smile and said, "So do ours."

From that time on, I have never doubted that there was a migration across the Bering Straight, whether over a land bridge or by traversing the sea. Just when that migration took place, there is no way to tell with certainty from the information now available. But that the migration took place was no longer a question in my mind. Certainly the crossing had been before Christ, perhaps by another one thousand years or more.

And today even though the cultures have developed differently over the centuries, there is an uncanny rapport that is remarkable.

The tour guide of our group was a sixty-two year-old man named Mr. Boiyo. It was Mr. Boiyo who had taken the initiative to set up the meeting with Ganbold at the Peace and Friendship Society. Mr. Boiyo was as pleasant a man as one ever hopes to meet, "a man of peace," such as described in the Bible. From our first meal, the Lord began to knit Mr. Boiyo and myself together as I busily wrote down all the Mongolian names of the food we were eating. This was not normal tourist behavior for the dinning room of the Bayan Gol Hotel.

Furthermore, besides jotting down the different foods at dinner, I was speaking a little Mongolian. At his age, working for the foreign service as he did, Mr. Boiyo had seen a lot of tourists in his career, most of them Russian and some from the Eastern European Communist countries, but he had never seen one who was trying to learn to speak his language.

In preparation for the trip, I had spent three weeks with headphones on, listening to tapes of an ancient Mongolian protocol of greeting, so that when we arrived in the country I could say, "Hello. How are you? How is your health? How is your family? How are your wife and children? How are your cattle? What's new?" I had memorized the greeting perfectly, which amazed the Mongols whom we met. After I would go through the introduction, they would look at me, and kind of tilt their head for a better look as if to say, "So you're an American." The fact was at that time in October of 1988, most Mongols had never seen a real live American, and all they knew about us was what Kruchev, Breshnev, and Andropov had told them, and you can imagine what that might have been!

However, the hard faced Russians had been there for seventy years and yet had never even bothered to learn to say hello, and yet here was an American saying hello in their language. The mere fact that I knew how to say hello, immediately began to melt the ice and dispel the propaganda and stereotyping of Americans they had heard from the Soviets. Mr. Boiyo literally took me around to government offices and said, "Speak Mongol, speak Mongol," and the people stood there amazed and began to look at me with that look that said, "Hey, what is this? We've never seen this before!"

If we think about it for a minute, we will recognize how important it is for a person to learn to say hello. Furthermore when a person has come to Christ, it usually began by someone else having said, "hello." The fact that someone had bothered to learn to say hello in Mr. Boiyo's language had made a crucial impression on him. At the same time it had put our spirit in an attitude of submission, which was then communicated subliminally so that he knew we truly loved him. We Christians should be the ones to take the initiative in conversation. It seems that back in the Garden of Eden, when communication was broken between man and God, that ever since then, it has been hard for people to communicate with each other as well. Without doubt, one of the devil's chief goals and strategies is to isolate people, and keep them from talking to one another. Equally as certain is that the Lord wants his people to break this barrier and be the ones to reach out and say, "hello."

The simple fact that our group was smiling was enough to set us apart from the dour Russians whom the Mongols had come to know over the years. The role we were trying to project was that of ambassadors of goodwill. My desire was to sow to the Spirit and hope that someday there would be a time to come back and water, and then harvest. We always asked permission before taking a picture, and Mr. Boiyo would say "Well of course, go right ahead, please, please," and day by day the Lord drew us closer and closer together. The fact that we asked, rather than just did what ever we pleased as some tourists might, was probably a little unusual. Could it be that we really respected him, and the Mongol's culture and traditions?

One day we said that we would like to meet some ordinary Mongolian people. Mr. Boiyo had a perplexed look on his face, which let me know this wasn't part of the itinerary, but also a look that let me know he was pleased and would do his best to fulfill my wish. It was then that the discovery was made that unknowingly I had brought something of a secret weapon along.

Tourists weren't shown into areas where common people lived, but instead were taken to the museums (which are interesting), the theaters, factories, government buildings, natural wonders, etc. But in keeping with the Communist mindset, contact with ordinary people was not allowed. However the next day as we returned from an outing, we were passing by some children walking home from school near one of the districts where people lived in the traditional Mongolian tent called a ger, and we asked if we could meet them. Mr. Boiyo ordered the bus to stop, but as we got out, the children were shy and began to run away. However Mr. Boiyo called and they stopped, and then bashfully stood together as I took out the secret weapon, which turned out to be a Polaroid Land camera. This was something Mongols had never seen before, not even Mr. Boiyo. Being able to give a photo of themselves to them right there on the spot was like magic. The camera worked wonderfully for meeting people, for in spite of their shyness, the camera soon drew crowds of adults and children alike, and everyone would watch in wonder as the magic took place and the images began to appear on the paper. This camera, which we take for granted in the West as old technology from the '60s, was still beyond the state of the art in Mongolia, and it produced the wonderful result of allowing us to get close to the people.

Since Mongols were nomads, it is hard for people who live in cities to understand them, for the simple fact is, they are different. They think differently, act differently, and their worldview is certainly different. To understand anything about Mongols, it is necessary to realize that up until just a couple of generations ago, the entire Mongol nation was totally nomadic. And therefore it is necessary to know something about the *ger* (rhymes with air), which is the ingenious Mongolian felt tent that has been around since before the time of Genghis Khan. The ger is one of the most distinctive aspects of Mongolian culture, and is clearly the ultimate home for a nomadic living in a cold climate. It offers protection from the wind and cold, yet can be put together or taken apart in less than an hour, and transported on the back of a camel.

Underneath the outer shell of canvas and felt, the ger has 'walls,' usually five of them, which are like a lattice or trellis, such as you might see on a porch in Switzerland, or Nova Scotia, or New Hampshire. This lattice like wall is approximately five feet high when stretched out like an accordion when the ger is erected, and about six feet tall when squeezed together for moving. When the ger is set up, the five walls are stretched out end to end, and neatly fit and tied together at their ends to form a circle, with the beginning of the first wall, and the end of the fifth wall, fitting into the door frame.

Around the top of the circumference of the walls, eighty-eight poles are then placed and extended inward and upward like spokes on a wagon wheel, where they are fit into a wheel like structure, which has eighty-eight holes around its edge into which the ends of the poles are inserted. Over this wooden skeleton, pieces of felt the height of the wall and four to five meters long are wrapped around the walls, and special cuts of the same felt material are sown together to form the roof. The wheel like structure at the very top is shaped much like a contact lens.

The felt covers only half of this wheel, and the other half is uncovered and has four triangular openings or windows framed into it, with one of these openings made with a hole for the stovepipe to pass through. Obviously before the twentieth century this opening was simply a smoke flap. But now most Mongols have small stoves, and burn either coal if

they can get it, or animal dung if they can't. When it rains the stovepipe is removed and the flap is pulled to cover the entire top of the ger. Some gers have six walls and a really large one will have eight. The smallest is a four-wall ger. Our family would live in a ger for three years and got to know them fairly well.

The last night we were in Mongolia Mr. Boiyo took us to the finals of the Mongolian National Folk Singing Contest. As we entered the theater, in one breathtaking moment, we found ourselves immersed deep into Mongolian culture. We were the only Westerners in the theater, which was filled with Mongols all dressed in their finest Mongolian dells. The dell is a sort of gown, or dress made of the finest silk, in an amazing array of brilliant colors; greens, maroons, yellows, blacks, whites, silvers, gold, and blues with sashes of orange, yellow, pink, or green around their waist. The music and atmosphere were like nothing we had ever experienced. Truly, Mongolia was like no other place on earth, a unique place where East met West in a marvelous harmony. We were overwhelmed! The architecture of the building was so overtly Western, all cream and crimson on the inside like Carnegie Hall, with huge majestic columns outside welcoming the concertgoers, and yet the content of the evening was so totally Mongolian. It was wonderfully culturally intoxicating.

The main instrument of the Mongols is a small cello-like instrument with two strings called a *morin khour*, played with a bow, and having a horse head carved at the top of the neck. *Morin* is the Mongolian word for horse, and *khour* means instrument. At times when it is played, it makes the most mournful of sounds, as if you were all alone out in the middle of the Gobi, crying out to the wind in the vastness of the night. At other times it is played like a galloping horse, running to catch the wind or whatever it is that's being pursued, or else to get away from the pursuer, as the case may be. Either way it is stirring, and through the music, a peculiar bonding was taking place inside my heart with these people of whom the world knew so little.

Mr. Boiyo had disappeared during the concert, and now, as we joined the applauding of the winners of the contest, he motioned from the side of the auditorium for us to come to him.

"Did you say you would like to buy a *morin khour*?" he asked.

"Of course."

"Follow me," said Mr. Boiyo and began to head for the doors leading backstage. We passed through the musicians and singers all dressed in their costumes who smiled and met the gaze of our eyes, welcoming us into the inner sanctums of Mongolian culture. Around a corner and down a long hall Mr. Boiyo led the way, and finally opened a door that brought us into the national workshop where the *morin khour*s were actually made.

"They leave tomorrow on a tour in the countryside and all they have is this one *morin khour* that has not been painted, but if you want it, they will make a case tonight." The *morin khour* was beautiful, even without the paint, and as I brought the bow across the strings there was that sound of the Gobi once again.

"I'll take it," I said, happy but subdued in realizing that people were actually going to work through the night to make the case. No service like that in America. Milt and I walked back to the hotel in silence, each of us reflecting on all that had happened that day.

We were due to leave at noon the next day, and it was hard to imagine what else could top what we had just experienced. We had forgotten for the moment that God was the one who had brought us here, that He had his own purposes for doing so, and that it was He who was in control.

> Do you not know? Have you not heard?
> the Everlasting God, the LORD,
> the Creator of the ends of the earth,
> does not become weary or tired,
> and His understanding, no one can fathom. (Is. 40:28)

And so it was that we were to discover that the Lord of all the earth was still at work that final morning we were in Mongolia.

I had gotten up early to take a last walk around the center of the city and pray. I had been careful during our visit not to say or do anything that would overtly identify us as Christians. After all, this was 1988, the Berlin wall was still up, and Communism very much alive. But now the Lord filled my heart so full as I walked across Sukhebaatar Square in the center of the city that I couldn't help but pray, "O Lord, open this country up," and I envisioned thousands of Mongols coming to Christ.

When I got back to the hotel I sensed the Holy Spirit saying, "Tell him about Me now," and as I walked in the door of the Bayan Gol, there stood Mr. Boiyo. It wasn't time to think or reason, only to obey, so I went over to Mr. Boiyo and said, "Could we step outside for just a minute, I have something I'd like to talk with you about." By this time, Mr. Boiyo and I had developed a pretty good friendship, so he said sure, and we headed for the doors.

Outside we walked over to a little waiting area out in front of the hotel with a few benches, and as we stood there I looked at my new found friend and asked, "What do you know about Jesus Christ?"

"Jesus Christ? Who is Jesus Christ?" Mr. Boiyo looked at me quizzically, then asked, "Does he live in the United States?"

"No, they killed Jesus Christ, but He came back to life." I replied and Mr. Boiyo was looking into my eyes.

"Really?" he said.

"Yes, and He's alive right now," I said.

And so I began the story of God becoming a man, and as I went on talking about Jesus and Mr. Boiyo heard the wonderful truth that God loved him, he was just overwhelmed. As he listened to the story of the crucifixion, and realized that God in the person of Jesus Christ had died for him, and that he could be forgiven, something broke inside of him. It must have been a terrible thing to have lived under the Communist system where the only way up the ladder was by stepping on someone else, a life of lies and deceit at every turn. Could all this be forgiven? The conviction of the Holy Spirit was strong. Mr. Boiyo was shaken. "All you have to do is believe," I said, and wrote out on a little piece of paper, "Jesus Christ forgives," and handed it to him.

There were not many Mongols at that time who knew English, and those who did usually worked for the KGB as tour guides. But even the KGB can be attracted to Jesus.

It was now time for breakfast, and we joined the rest of our group in the dining room inside the Bayan Gol. While we were eating, Mr. Boiyo was unusually quiet, as God was working in his heart. After breakfast, he and I had to go over to the Ulaanbaatar Hotel where the main tourist office was, and settle up the bill. There behind a big desk sat a little lady with her hair tied up in a bun at the back of her head, with eyes that could pierce through steel, and she wanted more money.

"No, no, no," I said, and she and I went round and round. This lady also knew English so Mr. Boiyo didn't have to translate. Then at a lull in our argument, I looked over at Mr. Boiyo sitting across the room and tears were streaming down his face. He looked up at me, and as our eyes met he reached into his coat pocket and brought out the piece of paper I had given him an hour before saying "Jesus Christ forgives." Mr. Boiyo looked down at the paper and then back up at me, and nodded his head with a little smile emerging through his tears. Glory to God, he was being saved right then and there!

I felt I had to do something so I asked the lady who'd had her head down pretending to concentrate on some papers, and saw none of this, if I could go to the restroom, knowing Mr. Boiyo would have to show me where it was. Once inside the restroom I asked him if he was all right. He looked at me and said, "I believe in Jesus Christ." This was incredible! But there he stood with a smile on his face and peace in his heart, confessing Jesus Christ, holding the little piece of paper, obviously being touched by God.

As we returned to the office I started to argue with the little tiger of a lady behind the desk again, but now Mr. Boiyo stopped me, took me outside the room and said, "No, no, no my boy. They won't let you come back in the country if you don't pay." His eyes were pleading so that there was nothing to do but give it up. So I went back in and paid an exorbitant amount for a little side trip we had taken, which I thought had been part of the tour package.

When we got back to the hotel we went upstairs and told Milt what had happened. We were carrying on praising the Lord so much that another member of our team, Phillip York, came in to find out what all the commotion was, and then all four of us began to rejoice together. Surely we were experiencing what the Apostle Paul must have felt in Philippi when the Lord opened the heart of Lydia. Finally, Milt presented Mr. Boiyo with a little pocket New Testament that he had brought along, and it was time to go to the train station.

By now Mr. Boiyo was in a daze, being pretty much overcome with all that was happening to him, and he was just barely able to get us to the train. But we found our carriage and coupes with their sleeping berths. The next thing we knew, time was running out and the conductor was calling for all guests to disembark from the train. We embraced in the narrow aisle, and then Mr. Boiyo stepped down onto the platform. We waved goodbye, and the train was moving, moving, taking us away from this place that I did not want to leave.

Milt and I sat in silence in our little compartment on the train as it made its way south towards China. We were more than a little stunned. Had the last few hours really happened? It had almost been like a dream. Serenely the words of a song from Psalm 45 came drifting into my mind, "My heart overflows with a good theme, I sing my song to the King, my tongue is nimble, my heart has a sweet sounding melody." And as the train chugged on down the track, something in my spirit knew that God was going to open up this country.

Mr. Boiyo, 1988

Chapter 3

What Do You Have to Tell Me?

"Pray on my behalf, that utterance may be given to me
to make known with boldness, the mystery of the gospel."
Ephesians 6:19-20.

In November of 1989, the Berlin wall came down, and by Christmas, all of Eastern Europe was free. Deliverance had not come from the hand of man. No military armies fought to free the people locked behind the iron curtain, but there had been a battle. In the book of Revelation we read of 'golden vials' that are used in heaven to collect the prayers of the saints. "In some profound and intricate way, the tears, travail and fastings of God's faithful are transformed upon their arrival in the spiritual dimension into pleasant and compelling odors; and as Rev. 8:1-6 suggests, the overflow of these prayer receptacles represents the tripwire of change.

When he broke the seventh seal,
there was silence in heaven for about half an hour.
And I saw the angels who stand before God;
and seven trumpets were given to them.
And another angel came and stood at the altar, holding a
golden censer: and much incense was given to him,
that he might add it to the prayers of all the saints upon
the golden altar which was before the throne.
And the smoke of the incense, with the prayers of the saints, went up
before God out of the angel's hand.
And the angel took the censer; and he filled it with the fire

of the altar and threw it to the earth; and there followed
peals of thunder and sounds and flashes of lightning and an earthquake.
And seven angels who had the seven trumpets prepared themselves to sound them.

In a response to this remarkable passage Heaven itself falls silent. The heavenly hosts and celestial spheres suspend their ceaseless singing so that the prayers of the saints on earth can be heard. The seven angels of destiny cannot blow the signal of the next times to be until an eighth angel gathers these prayers... and mingles them with the incense of the altar. Silently they rise to the nostrils of God. Human beings have intervened in the heavenly liturgy. The uninterrupted flow of consequences is dammed up for a moment. New alternatives become feasible. The unexpected becomes suddenly possible, because God's people on earth have invoked heaven, the home of the possible, and they have been heard. What happens next, happens because people prayed. The message is clear. History belongs to the intercessors."[5]

In January 1990, I began planning my second trip into Mongolia. Then suddenly on March 11, the dynamics of the democratic movement of Eastern Europe, which had also begun in Mongolia the preceding fall, reached their final culmination. The zealous young man named Zorig, with a bullhorn in his hand, led the demonstrators in Sukhebaatar Square. Finally, the President and Parliament of Mongolia resigned, and Communist ideology no longer ruled in Mongolia. The world seemed to be really changing.

In light of this new development, I began to seek the Lord, to see what He might have us to do. The answer was not what I expected. I had to call my wife, Laura, to come and pray with me because I thought I heard the Lord saying that He wanted us to go to Mongolia and witness to the new Mongolian government leaders. As we rose to our feet from praying, Laura agreed, and said, "I believe that is what the Lord is saying." And so every day we continued to pray and each time the word was clear that the Lord indeed wanted us to witness to the new government leaders in

5   George Otis Jr. *The Last of the Giants*, (Tarrytown, New York: Chosen Books, 1991) pp.47-48

Mongolia. But how was this to come about? There were no churches or missionaries yet in the country, and only one believer that we knew of.

In our efforts to get Native Americans to go to Mongolia, we were living on the edge of the Navajo reservation outside of Gallup, New Mexico, and I was driving a school bus for Rehoboth Christian School. Two weeks before we were due to leave for Mongolia, I was taking the boarding school students from the town of Shiprock home for the weekend when the small still voice of the Lord began to reveal to me the plan that would bring our testimony and His word to the new government leaders in Mongolia.

That night I was on the phone with some influential people around the country, who in turn gave me the phone number for Senator William Armstrong of Colorado. The following Monday morning I was on the phone and the conversation went something like this.

"Senator Armstrong's office, may I help you?"

"Hello, my name is Rick Leatherwood and I'm with a mission called Mongolian Enterprises International, and I am taking a team of people into Mongolia in about ten days, and I need to talk to Senator Armstrong before we leave if possible. Would he be in the country?"

"Just a moment please."

I was calling from our little mobile home at Rehoboth just outside of Gallup when the next thing I heard was, "Hello Bill Armstrong here." Without any warning, the secretary had put me right through!

"Hello Senator Armstrong, my name is Rick Leatherwood and I am with a mission called Mongolian Enterprises and I am taking a team into Outer Mongolia in about ten days."

"Wow, that sounds exciting Rick."

"Yes sir, Senator Armstrong, and what we believe the Lord wants us to do is to witness to the new government leaders of Mongolia and see if we can influence them towards religious freedom in their country."

"My that does sound exciting!"

"Yes it is, and I am wondering, Senator Armstrong, if you would mind writing me a letter addressed to the new President of Mongolia which I can take with us and hopefully use to gain an audience with their leaders?"

"Well, I don't see why not. That sounds good to me, Rick. Say, I'm in my car right now so I'll forward you back to the office and my assistant will take down the information needed for the letter and we'll see what we can do."

Now isn't that how all telephone conversations go when speaking to United States Senators? I didn't know Bill Armstrong from Adam, and he didn't know me, but we both knew Jesus Christ and in this case, that was all that it took. I had caught Senator Armstrong on the beltway riding in his limousine back to his office, while I was tucked into my little five-by-five office in the corner of the bedroom of our mobile home in Rehoboth, New Mexico. God is so good.

The second trip was scheduled for early June, and this time the Lord called members of four different Native American tribes to go with us, from the Kiowa, Cocopaw, Winnebago, and another from the Navajo.

I was laying out the vision of taking Native Americans to Mongolia before a packed house of the Frontier Fellowship at the US Center for World Mission with Flint Poolaw of the Kiowa tribe there with me and the room was just electrified. Suddenly a woman stood up right in the middle of my presentation and said I'll give $1000 to send that young man to Mongolia. Her name was Virginia Bryant, mother of David Bryant, president of Concerts Of Prayer International. People were really onboard with this vision.

Also one of our supporters felt strongly that Laura should go to Mongolia this time and gave the money needed for her to make the trip. Our one-year old daughter, Jessica, was still nursing, so she would have to go as well, but at her age there was no expense for her ticket.

As we prepared to leave on the trip, I sent a short one-page letter out to everyone for whom I had an address, announcing our trip into Mongolia. I knew from my first trip that fear would be our greatest opponent, and so I asked everyone to pray a verse from Ephesians for us, "and pray on my behalf, that utterance may be given to me in the opening of my mouth, to make known *with boldness* the mystery of the gospel for which I am an ambassador in chains; that in proclaiming it, I may speak boldly as I ought to speak." (Eph. 6:19-20)

Naturally I was hoping that Mr. Boiyo would be our tour guide, but even before we got off the train, a young man popped his head through the doorway and was introducing himself, "Hello, my name is Basanhu. I will be your guide while you are here in Mongolia." I was disappointed, but there was nothing that could be done. It was June 3rd and a little cold. The train had gotten in to Ulaanbaatar about 4:00 in the afternoon, some three hours late, so that there was nothing for our team to do but go to the hotel (the same one I was in before), clean up, eat dinner, pray, and go to bed. But, of course, even this was quite an experience in itself for the members of our team, as everything was of the Mongolian culture and therefore even a common thing like dinner was a new adventure.

The next morning we took an in-country flight to the ancient capitol of Mongolia called Khara Khorum that dates back to the days of the great Khans. It didn't take a lot of imagination to visualize the vast Mongol army and their horses camped in the broad green valley next to the Orhon River, with the Hangai Mountains on the far side providing game to help feed the army. The huge Buddhist monastery at this site was built in 1578, more than two hundred years after the Mongol Empire collapsed. Somehow it had escaped being destroyed by the Communists but was in need of some repair. This is one of the most famous tourist attractions in Mongolia, and upon seeing the monastery, whose walls are eighteen feet high and enclose an area of nearly eight acres, you really get a glimpse at how pervasive Buddhism had been in Mongolia. All that is left from the days of the Khans is a huge stone tortoise about four hundred yards to the south of the monastery. It seemed like a strategic place to pray, and so we gathered around and prayed against the powers and principalities of darkness that held the Mongolian people in bondage. Little did I know that in the years to come I would return many times to this very place to pray, binding the strongman of the enemy and pulling down his strongholds until I was hoarse.

As we returned to the tourist camp from our visit to Khara Khorum, Jim Tohtsonie the Navajo pointed out which horses we saw along the way were mares, which were geldings, and which were stallions. Jim's family still lived close to the land in northern Arizona and he grew up around horses and sheep much like the Mongols. He spoke easily and yet with such authority and knowledge that everyone was pretty impressed with Jim's explanations.

Ancient walls at Khara Khorum

The next day we were on our way to a picnic at a famous waterfall when suddenly I realized this was not what we had come to do. "Stop the bus," I blurted out, "we didn't come to Mongolia to go sightseeing." I looked at our tour guide Basanhu and said, "Would it be all right if we didn't go on this picnic?" Everyone was naturally wondering what was going on. Understandably they had come on a trip that might include things like picnics and they were prepared to go with the flow. But we were on a mission and I felt a keen sense that we needed to be creating the flow. Up until now there was nothing that would have tipped Basanhu off that this tour group was any different from what he had normally known, except that we were Americans. But no doubt the wheels were spinning in his mind as he calmly said, "You're the boss," and ordered the driver to turn around.

When we got back to the tourist camp, our team began to relax by playing some volleyball with a group of Russian tourists. So I invited Basanhu into my ger and we sat down on stools together in front of a low Mongolian table in the middle of the room.

It was then I showed Basanhu the letter I had brought with me from Senator William Armstrong of the United States Congress. The letter with its letterhead identifying it as from a United States Senator was addressed to the President of Mongolia, and its contents strongly urged the new President and his government to allow religious freedom in Mongolia. I handed it to Basanhu who read the letter and looked up a few minutes later wide-eyed and in total amazement. Basanhu looked over at me and said, "I will do everything I can to get you to the leaders of my country." As only God can arrange things, it turned out that Basanhu had heard the gospel from another American tourist, and as he heard the word of Christ, faith was born in his heart and he believed. Basanhu was a true believer!

The next morning we flew back to Ulaanbaatar and Basanhu and I went to pay a visit to the Mongolian Ministry of Foreign Affairs. Upon entering the front door we were shown into a small waiting room and given some tea. A few minutes later a man came in to see us. After cordial introductions, we shared that I was here in Mongolia for the next week and pulled out the letter from Senator Armstrong. The man to whom we were talking could not speak any English but could tell from the letterhead that it was a message of importance, as Basanhu began to explain that it was from a United States Senator. At this the man looked up, asked us to wait for a moment and excused himself. He came back about ten minutes later with another man obviously of a higher rank, who asked if it would be possible for me to leave the letter with them so that they could have it translated, and they would get back to us for another meeting. That was fine with me, and so Basanhu and I took our leave feeling things had gone well.

From talking with various members of our team, Basanhu had learned that one of the Indians on our team was something of a cowboy. Indians have great respect for American cowboy culture as it essentially revolves around horses, rather than politics. Milt Shirleson who had come with me to Mongolia back in 1988, was the head of an organization in Arizona called Cowboys for Christ and had written to the director of the Mongolian Horse Association informing him that our group was coming. When we got back to the hotel, the Association's director whom Basanhu had contacted was waiting to meet us with an invitation for our team to come to a day of horsemanship out in the countryside two days later.

Our team spent the next day visiting the Mongolian Museum of Natural History, which really is spectacular, with lots of Mongolian artifacts, including a great number of things from the days of Genghis Khan. The climax was a thirty-five foot tall skeleton of a Tyrannosaurus Rex found in the Gobi Desert. As this was standing in their museum well before the days of Jurassic Park, it was pretty impressive.

The following day after breakfast, a small bus came to meet us at the hotel. We drove for about an hour and a half through beautiful Mongolian countryside dotted with gers, and thousands and thousands of sheep, goats, horses, and yaks, before pulling off the main road to where the horse demonstration would take place. Imagine our surprise as we stepped off the bus, less than three months after the democratic revolution of March 11, 1990, and were greeted by television cameras, newspaper reporters, magazine photographers, journalists, and government officials! It wasn't until then that we realized that the whole Mongolian nation was aware that our little party was in the country, and that they were fascinated by these Native Americans who were so much like themselves.

Hundreds of yak were grazing nearby, when all of a sudden, three hundred horses came over the hill in a stampede and the show was on. Navajo Jim Tohtsonie pulled on his boots, donned his straw cowboy hat, and got out his lariat. However the equipment that he needed most was a western saddle. Nevertheless Jim was game to try a Mongol saddle, which is pretty narrow and sits the rider considerably higher than a western saddle, and is pretty difficult for most westerners to ride. But Jim climbed aboard and trotted around a bit getting used to the small Mongolian horse and the high saddle, before letting out his lariat.

The TV cameras were rolling and Jim roped his first eight horses in a row without a miss. If ever there was anybody who loves a rodeo,

it is Mongols. The mere fact that we were willing and wanting to do something with horses put us in high esteem with them. It was fantastic, and the more I watched the young Mongol wranglers ride, really boys sixteen or seventeen years old, who were riding hard to keep all the horses in close to the TV cameras so that everything could be filmed, I thought to myself, "We don't have anything to teach these people about horsemanship! These Mongols are without a doubt the finest horsemen in the world! These were the people who had conquered the world on horseback!"

Furthermore watching these young riders was something like watching a great artist paint. It was like poetry in motion. They stand high in the saddle. They don't sit. They stand, and they just lean and bend with the horse as it cuts or makes a turn. And yet I have never seen a Mongol fall from his horse. You have to wonder, how can they do that! But riding horses was what Mongols were all about. And so I walked over to the old herdsman to whom all of these horses belonged and asked if I might ride. Immediately the old herdsman signaled one of the young riders to come over to where we were standing. The old man spoke, and the young man dismounted and handed me the reigns.

I put my foot in the stirrup, my knee in the horse's shoulder, grabbed the pummel and mounted in one motion. The last thing I heard as I slapped the rump of the horse was Basanhu shouting, "Don't go too fast." But I was off like the wind at a full gallop. I hadn't told anybody on the team, but eleven years before, I had been a cowboy raising horses. Just as horses had been at the center of Mongolian and Native American culture for centuries, they were my whole life back then, and there is just something about horses that bonds horse people together. Sure enough, when I trotted back to the group a few minutes later, I sensed a new respect from all the Mongols. They seemed both amazed and pleased. Another American who could ride, and fast!

After a few hours of demonstrating various ways of American and Mongolian horsemanship, we all sat down together. The Mongols had prepared a kind of cultural exchange where some Mongolian hostesses dressed in pink dells came out and served us tea and gave us each a little gift. The government official then made a speech and presented the team with various tokens of recognition, and everyone was having a good time.

Then Ollie Heth, who was all dressed up in a beautiful white beaded buckskin dress of the Winnebago tribe, asked if it would be all right for her to dance? "Of course" the Mongols all said, "yes, please," and things continued to build and were becoming more and more interesting all the time. Ollie walked over to my wife Laura and Starla Shetler, who was another member of our team and asked Laura and Starla if they knew how to sing the Lord's Prayer, and it turned out both of them had sung the entire song in church before.

The next thing we knew Laura and Starla were singing, and Ollie was portraying the Lord's Prayer in beautiful, graphic Indian sign language. It was actually a dance that was telling a story, all at the same time. The whole performance was extraordinary, powerful, and amazing, and all of it was being filmed and translated for Mongolian television! It was shown on national television the following month during the *Naadam* festival, one of the most important celebrations of the Mongol's culture!

After the dance and the presentations were over, the Mongolian government officials got into their Russian jeeps and headed back to town, and I was wondering if we should do the same when the old herdsman who was hosting the day came up to me with our translator Basanhu.

"This man wants to know if he can ask you a question," said Basanhu.

"Sure."

The old herdsman looked at me and said something.

"He wants you to know that he's not a Communist," said Basanhu.

The old man spoke again and Basanhu translated, "He wants you to know that he's not a Buddhist."

The old man spoke once more. "He wants to know what you have to tell him."

Well you might have to wait a lifetime to be asked a question like that. But there it was, so I looked at the old man and said to Basanhu, "Tell him I'd like to talk to him about a man who rose from the dead."

Basanhu translated this into Mongolian, and the old man paused for just a moment and then spoke again and Basanhu looked up with a smile on his face and said, "He wants to know if you would like to stay for dinner."

And so we all relaxed and began to enjoy real Mongolian culture. We watched as the old herdsman searched through his flock for just the right sheep to butcher. And we stood in utter amazement as the old man cut the belly of the sheep instead of the throat. Then he reached in with his hand and did something, we didn't know what, but a few moments later the sheep was dead. Well you live and learn something everyday.

The neighbors came over and invited us to their place to drink some *airag*. *Airag* is fermented mare's milk and the national drink of Mongolia, and since it is mentioned in *The Secret History of the Mongols*, it's been around awhile. In the summer, the Mongols will milk their horses five times a day and put all the milk into a big barrel or leather pouch, where they stir the fresh milk into the old and let the bacteria cause the milk to ferment. The alcoholic content is probably less than 1%, and you'd get sick before you ever got drunk. It tastes something like a mixture of champagne and buttermilk. I learned to like it early on by taking a big swig rather than trying to sip it. Basanhu came up to me and said, "I have never seen a tour group get this close to the Mongol people. Your group is very special."

Dinner was ready just as the sun was setting, and we all gathered into the old herdsman's ger. All of the magazine photographers and journalists had stayed, along with a few newspaper reporters, and together with the herdsman's family and neighbors, we were about thirty-five people squeezed inside the ger. They indicated that I was to sit on the far side of the ger, directly opposite from the door, which is the traditional seat of honor. So there we were, actually about to have dinner in a Mongolian ger. It was amazing. There were no plates, no silverware, no salad, no vegetables, just meat. This was the real thing, because this was all they had. There are few pretenses among Mongols, and their culture, even at the close of the twentieth century, was remarkably intact. Natural would be the best way to think of it, especially in the countryside, where it had changed little over thousands of years.

They brought in a pot of steaming meat and set it down right in front of me. As the guest of honor, it was my job to cut up the meat, but when I tried to touch it, it was so hot it burned my fingers and I jerked back. The Mongols all laughed, everyone thoroughly enjoying the moment at my expense. But the meat was scalding hot! I tried again with no better results, as everyone laughed all the more. So a big man came over, grabbed the knife out of my hand, picked up a piece of meat and whacked off a big piece with a grin and looked at me as if to say that though the meat was hot, he was no wimp like me. But I was glad to be relieved of the job and grinned back just as big, and we all laughed together. As he cut the meat, he would hand the piece he had just cut to someone who would accept it with both hands cupped together. At this point Navajo Jim Tohtsonie spoke up and said, "This is the same way we Indians eat our meat," meaning both the way it was cooked and served. Basanhu translated what Jim had said into Mongolian, and all the Mongols looked at Jim and the other Native Americans and nodded approvingly.

After this, for the second course, they cut the liver into thin strips and put a piece of fat on it, and passed this around the room in the same manner as before. And once again Jim spoke up saying, "This is exactly the same way we Navajo eat our sheep." And when Basanhu translated this time, it was as if someone had plugged an electric wire into the ger and the whole room took on a surreal atmosphere. It was not hard at to imagine this whole meal taking place in an Indian tepee, or in a Navajo *hogan,* which is about the same size and shape as a ger.

The whole scene seemed transcendent in the dim light, the mood was rich, the odors pungent, and we were drinking deeply of the moments, when the old herdsman, who was seated to my left, suddenly got up and walked across the room and out the door, only to reappear a minute later. He stopped in the doorway and was holding a baby lamb in his arms. He spoke, and Basanhu looked at me and said, "The lamb is a gift to your daughter," Little did we know that in Mongolian culture we had greatly honored these people by bringing our little one-year old Jessica into their home.

Everywhere we went Jessica, with her strawberry blond hair and blue eyes opened doors into people's hearts. In one place we went, a lady stayed up all night and sewed a little Mongolian dell for Jessica, which she was now wearing. I stood to receive the gift on behalf of our daughter and walked to the center of the ger. After I took the lamb into my arms, I said, "Thank you so very much for this gift. This is truly a great honor, and we have had such a wonderful time with you here today. You have made us feel welcome, and it has truly been good to be with you. And the gift of this lamb is very special. And ah, would it be all right if I told a story about another lamb?"

The old herdsman and all the Mongols eagerly nodded their heads with loud exclamations, and everyone seemed to be saying, 'Yes, tell us a story.' So we sat down again, with me holding the lamb in my lap. It was important that I connect with the first line, to bond and find some common ground, and so looking around the ger at the people I said, "Back in the days of Genghis Khan, didn't the Mongolian people call God, Tenger?" Basanhu translated and all the Mongols nodded that this was true. Their anticipation had not been disappointed. We were talking about God. Their eyes were wide, and so it was that I began to tell the story of Jesus, the Lamb of God.

"One day about 2000 years ago, Tenger became a man and that man's name was Jesus Christ. And this man Jesus Christ did things that no other man has ever done. He made blind people see, and he made sick people well. Then to prove to everyone that He was really Tenger... He allowed Himself to be killed, and for three days He was dead... and then He came back to life." You could have heard a pin drop as these people listened to the words of eternal life for the first time. I spoke of the incarnation. I told of Christ's life on earth, and explained the sacrifice that He had made as the Lamb of God to take away the sins of the world. I spoke of death as the common enemy of all people everywhere, and the wonderful truth that the God who created the world was a God of love, did not create men to die, but to live, and finally brought the message back to Jesus as the Lamb of God. The Mongols sat in silence and listened. It was almost unbelievable, what they had just heard.

"Who would like to accept the sacrifice of the Lamb of God?" I asked, and all around the room hands went up. I had not asked them to raise their hands. It was a spontaneous, response of their own. Here was good news, and like most simple people, they could understand it and wanted it. "All right, let's all stand up," I said, and we stood up together, the newspaper reporters, the magazine photographers, the journalists, the old herdsman, his friends and family, everyone. "Now let's take each other's hands," and so we all clasped hands and I prayed a prayer of salvation. Basanhu translated it into Mongolian, and the Mongols all repeated the prayer. I said amen, and then fittingly enough the old herdsman began to speak. "The Lamb that has been given to your daughter, will not be killed, but will lead a natural life, as a reminder to all of us, of the Lamb of God."

It is hard to find the right words to describe that moment. Our team was hugging everyone in the ger, speaking to the people with joy that was understood though the words were not. The euphoria was transcendent. It was now quite late, and time for us to leave. We boarded the little bus along with the other people from town who had stayed, the newspaper reporters, the magazine journalists and photographers. I was exhausted. It had been a big day, and together with Laura and Jessica, I sat down in one of the seats near the front of the bus and just kind of collapsed and tried to decompress a bit. But in the back of the bus a lively discussion began between the rest of our team and the Mongol journalists and photographers, who all had lots of questions.

One of them asked, "What happened to me back there?"

"What do you mean?" replied the Native Americans.

"You know, when we took each other's hands, what was it that happened to me?" And so all the way back to Ulaanbaatar the Native Americans who are wonderful teachers, shared with their long lost brethren who had just been found, just what had happened to them back there.

CHAPTER 4

Baptism

"We were therefore buried with him through baptism into death,
in order that, just as Christ was raised from the dead
through the glory of the Father, we too may live a new life."
Romans 6:4

The next morning we ate a late breakfast and Basanhu was there to join us. Somehow we got into talking about all of the things that had happened so far on our trip and just how remarkable it all had been. But it was something that was said almost in passing that turned out to be the catalyst to an important part of Basanhu's life.

The Indians were talking about our time in China, and of getting on the train and crossing the Gobi Desert. I had told them kind of casually, having been on that train once before, that at the border we would have to get off the train and they would change the wheels on the train. Everyone looked at me as if I had two heads. "What do you mean they're going to change the wheels on the train?" they asked incredulously, just as I did, the first time I heard that.

"Just wait and see," I teased, knowing there was really nothing more I could add and they would just have to wait until we got to the border to see it for themselves. It is kind of mind boggling to think about, and even more to see it done.

Well, there was one significant detail about our stop at the border, besides passports and visas and customs officials, etc. and that was the fact that they locked all the doors to the bathrooms on the train when it was stopped in front of the station. We didn't learn this until we got back on the train, thinking we were about to leave, and having drunk lots of pop and stuff at the border. After the normal two to three hour stop at the border where the wheels are changed due to the difference in the gage in the tracks between China and Mongolia, and the checking of visas and going through customs, we got back on the train but the train didn't leave. Laura had luckily gone to the bathroom just before we got to the border and she was fine and went to sleep with Jessica, but for three more hours we were stopped in the middle of the night with the bathroom doors locked and no way to get off the train again as they had locked those doors as well, and all the rest of us were really, really needing to use the bathroom.

Now a week later we all sat at the breakfast table laughing and recalling how we had paced up and down the corridor of the train, waiting for it to get moving so that the bathroom doors could be unlocked. Suddenly Basanhu gave a little jerk as if he'd just heard his mother call, and he looked at us all wide eyed in a way that made everybody stop and look at him. While we had all been sitting there laughing and joking about what had happened, Basanhu had been figuring out what all of this meant on his end of things.

Finally he said, "Do you remember that your train was three hours late getting into Ulaanbaatar?" We all nodded as that was what we had just been talking about. "If your train had been on time, I would not be your tour guide." We all took this in rather gravely as it was plain that Basanhu was obviously appointed by God to be our tour guide. He then told us how his phone had not been working for a whole week before we arrived and that the state travel agency had not been able to get in touch with him and he had no idea we were coming. Then on the day of our arrival just an hour before our train arrived, his phone started working again and he got a call to get down to the train station and meet a tour group of Americans. Had our train been on time, another person would have been assigned to be our guide. Had Basanhu's phone been working the previous week, he would possibly not have been our tour guide but would have been assigned to another group instead of ours. We distinctly saw the sovereignty of God's hand.

While Basanhu was telling us his story I could see the wheels in his mind were spinning and he finally said, "You are not in control of this," meaning all that had been happening. And we all just kind of sat there in silence and our lack of words confirmed what he was thinking, that no, we were not in control of what was happening. And Basanhu knew perfectly well that he wasn't in control of things, and I think it must have all just dawned on him at that moment that it was God who was in control of everything that was going on. This had unmistakably come like a revelation to Basanhu, and he looked up at me with new understanding and said, "I'd like to be baptized. Would you baptize me?"

Acts 1:7 teaches that the times and the seasons are in the authority of God, and other Scriptures tell us that it is He who causes His light to shine in the darkness, who raises up and puts down, and makes rivers flow in the desert. I guess we might add that He causes trains to mysteriously stop in the middle of the night. One sows, another waters, but God gives the increase. Someone plans a trip and others give resources for messengers to go, but it is God who is at work, producing even unexplainable bureaucratic delays at border crossings, to will and to do His good pleasure. And so we continued to witness God's opening of Mongolia. How easily we forget that He is the one who is the author of life and desires that none should perish, and is moving throughout the earth that His name might be known among the nations. How important it is for us all to remember that we are not on a trip, we are on a mission. Our God is a missionary God.

I naturally said I would be glad to baptize him, and then added, "There is another man here who needs to be baptized too. Do you know a Mr. Boiyo?" and now it was Basanhu's turn to be surprised and raise his eyebrows. He said yes, he knew Mr. Boiyo very well. "May I ask you to give Mr. Boiyo a call and tell him I am here and would like to see him?"

A few hours later we were back for lunch in the dining hall at the Bayan Gol Hotel and were seated at a table at the entrance of the hall. From my vantage point I could see out into the hallway that led into the dining room, and suddenly he was there. The hallway was a little dark, but nevertheless I knew it was Mr. Boiyo, and I was up on my feet in a moment.

It seemed as though he were hesitating, a little uncertain of himself from what must have been a surprising phone call from Basanhu, and so I went out into the hallway to greet him. His first words were, "Please, you tell me more about Jesus Christ."

It was so good to see him again and to hear these words come out of his mouth. He told us how he had taken the little Bible Milt Shirleson had given to him nineteen months before and had put it on his nightstand where he had read it every night before going to bed. We ate, we talked, we laughed, we enjoyed the goodness of God. And so I told Mr. Boiyo about the meaning of baptism, that it was a sign that he belonged to Jesus, and he said yes, he too wanted to be baptized.

This was Saturday, and Basanhu made the arrangements for the bus that had taken us to the countryside the day before to be available for us the following day. And so we spent the rest of the day preparing for the baptism. I wanted everyone on the team to participate in some way, with a Scripture, a song, a prayer, or a blessing of some kind. It seemed fitting that the baptism would be on a Sunday.

The next day dawned clear and bright, and Basanhu brought his wife, Alima, and their son Ananda, to witness his baptism. And so together with Basanhu and his family, Mr. Boiyo and our team of nine, we climbed aboard the bus and journeyed outside of town about an hour's drive to a secluded place on the banks of the Tol River. Leaving the bus and the driver at the end of the road, we walked on downstream a few minutes, looking for a back eddy with a deep enough pool and sure enough as we rounded a bend in the river there was just the right spot.

There we sang, we read Scripture, we prayed, we worshipped and rejoiced in the wonder of it all. We drank deeply of the moments that followed and the goodness of God in allowing us to take part in what He was now doing in Mongolia. Each person present contributed in some way, one with a prayer, another with a song, another reading a Scripture.

Jim Lopez of the Cocopaw tribe joined me in the water to help with the baptism, and once in the river we asked Basanhu what he believed about Jesus Christ.

Basanhu said he believed Jesus Christ was the Son of God and that he was the Savior of the world. And so in the name of the Father, and the Son, and the Holy Ghost, we baptized Basanhu.

Then it was Mr. Boiyo's turn. Mr. Boiyo took off his shoes and rolled up his trousers, and stepped into the water. "Can you tell us Mr. Boiyo about your faith in Jesus Christ?" I asked, and Mr. Boiyo said simply, "He has forgiven my sins. I believe He is God's Son."

"Because of your faith in Jesus Christ, Mr. Boiyo, we baptize you in the name of the Father, and the Son, and the Holy Spirit."

What an incredible step of faith these two men had taken. They had been a little nervous and even a bit scared, but they were willing, and the ice had been broken. What would be the consequences? Would there be others to follow in the days to come? Here they were, the first of their people within their country's borders in modern history, to step forward in obedience to follow Christ in baptism.

Only nineteen months earlier, I had shared with Mr. Boiyo the news that the nature of the true God was love and that Christ had risen from the dead. These two aspects of Christianity are the most important and outstanding features of our faith. What if this were not so? What if God were not love? The human race would be in big trouble. We would all be lost. What if God were capricious as in Buddhism? No grace. No mercy. Just judgment from a being whom it would be impossible to please. This is the fear that Buddhists around the world must live with, whether in Mongolia, Tibet, Burma, Thailand, or wherever. The angry masks we see them wearing in their dances are the elite of their many gods. Their faces are distorted and horrid, and with cruel looking swords that are carried by the dancers, they challenge any and all who dare approach their authority. What if this was the way God really was? There would be no hope. How good to know the truth… God is love.

The other dynamic that makes Christianity what it is, and sets Christ apart from all other religious leaders the world has ever known, is the resurrection. We rightly say that a person needs to be born again. But how does this happen? Peter tells us that God "causes us to be born again through the resurrection of Jesus Christ," (1 Peter 1:3). We claim that Jesus Christ is the Son of God. How do we know? Paul tells us in his letter to the Romans, "He was declared the son of God by the resurrection from the dead," (Romans 1:4). Buddha is dead. Mohammed is dead. And Jesus? He was also dead, but He came back to life, doing what no one else had ever done or could do, to prove the things He had said were true.

And so there we were, celebrating the new life that God has given to us all through His Son. We ate a lunch together by the banks of the river, basking in the sun, trying to comprehend the significance of what had just taken place. Laura and Starla visited with Basanhu's wife, Alima, the best they could, but of course Basanhu, or Mr. Boiyo had to be their translator. The date was June 10, 1990.

That afternoon, one of the newspaper journalists who had been present that night in the ger and had been the one who had asked what had happened to him came by to continue the friendship that had begun. His name was Munkhjargal, and he obviously had a bright mind and was wanting to know more. He spoke English quite well, being self-taught with a natural gift in language, and so he was able to communicate with our group without the help of a translator.

Flint Poolaw of the Kiowa nation, a big but soft spoken and gentle man, opened up and told a traditional story of his people. It was about ten grandmothers who were really ten buffalo hide bags that their medicine men would carry around. The bags were a sign of the medicine men's power, and Flint shared that as a boy he had once strongly believed in their power and their traditional religion. But all the medicine in their medicine bags could not answer his questions about life, and he found no peace until he met Jesus Christ.

Munkhjargal had clearly been touched by God and it was good for him to hear these further testimonies of how Christ had come into other people's lives. Munkhjargal was a young intellectual who was hungry for knowledge and truth, and perhaps was comprehending more than many the changes that would be coming to his country, understanding that it had just experienced a major turning point in its history.

Basanhu had asked if he could invite some of his friends over to the hotel to talk with us. Naturally, we agreed and I particularly wanted the Native Americans to take the lead and have them be the ones to preach the gospel that night, so at dinner we went over our plans for the evening and how we would proceed.

Basanhu's friends included an artist, a businessman, and a schoolteacher. We looked at some of the artist's paintings which were quite good, and listened to some ideas of the businessman of how we could all become rich, but the school teacher just stood and waited. He alone seemed to have some understanding as to the import of the evening. It seemed to be an evening for the men, so Ollie, Starla and Laura just popped in to say hello, then left us to ourselves.

The Native Americans had decided that Flint Poolaw from the Kiowa Nation would once again be the first to share. Flint began to tell us the story of his childhood. He told of the hardship his family had lived through as a result of alcohol. Little did he know the businessman was a chronic alcoholic. What a precious and tender time Flint gave us as he unfolded his tragic, then wonderful story. He explained how he too had become an alcoholic like his father, and then stated that Jesus Christ had changed all that and set him free.

Next Jim Tohtsonie told a bit of his family history, and really, the history of all the Navajo as they too struggled to make it amidst the ravages of alcohol among their people. And then I shared the story of Jesus with these men.

It was the teacher in the back of the room who seemed to understand more than the other two what was being said. Afterwards he asked many questions and it was obvious that there was a hunger in him to know more. His name was Boldbaatar, and he had an easy smile that he was not afraid to share. But I sensed this night was a time of sowing, rather than of reaping, and so we parted late that evening with a warm handshake and a smile of excitement coming from Boldbaatar's eyes. Let what he had heard incubate in his mind and I felt sure he would come to Christ.

The next morning, Monday, we heard back from the Ministry of Foreign Affairs with the news that they would see us on Wednesday at noon in response to the letter from Senator Armstrong. We were scheduled to leave on Thursday, so this would be an interesting climax to our trip. Next an invitation came from Ganbold at the Peace and Friendship Association, who had met Milt Shirleson back in 1988, saying he would like to host a reception in honor of the Native Americans, also on Wednesday. And then a third call came from the Mongolian State University, requesting a visit from Dr. Stanley Block, a college professor who was the eldest member of our party. With our train scheduled to leave on Thursday, we were now hurtling towards an exciting finish.

Since things were developing so quickly, it seemed best to concentrate on what lay ahead on Wednesday, focusing on what the Lord had already given us, rather than going out and trying to initiate anything new. Fortunately, the meeting at the Peace and Friendship Association was scheduled for two o'clock that afternoon, and the one at the University for five o'clock, so none of our meetings conflicted with the others. But first was the meeting at noon with the Ministry of Foreign Affairs.

We took the rest of Monday and Tuesday to walk around the city parks, shop at the State Department Store, visit Sukhebaatar Square, rest, pray, think, and prepare. Various Mongols whom we had met, came by again such as the teacher Boldbaatar, and Munkhjargal the journalist. Boldbaatar whom was known simply as Bold, could not speak English (yet), but seemed to want to just be with us, so we welcomed him for a meal.

On Wednesday morning we once again had our little school bus to ferry us around for that final day, and as we arrived at the Ministry of Foreign Affairs, I let the others go on ahead so that I could have a final word with Basanhu.

"When we go inside, I want you to introduce our group as goodwill ambassadors of Jesus Christ." Basanhu raised his eyebrows a bit in apprehension so I added, "We have nothing to hide. This is who we are and what we believe. He has been good for us and He will be good for you." Basanhu smiled as here was the truth. Could it have been that the prayers for the boldness asked for in Eph. 6:19 were continuing to be answered? As Solomon said, "To everything there is a season, and a time for every purpose under heaven." There are times when it is best to be discreet, and there are times to be open, and candid… to step out in faith and trust God. This was one of those times.

We were ushered into a large room on the second floor with a long table in the middle, and ten chairs on each side. Several Mongolian foreign ministers were already waiting in the room and they met us cordially, welcoming the Native Americans and thanking us all for coming to Mongolia. No doubt the story of the horse demonstration had been reported along with its accompanying ceremony, which had gone so well.

And so our team of nine, which included the four tribes of Native Americans, Dr. Block, Starla, Laura, Jessica, and I, sat down on one side of the table with Basanhu, while the Mongolian ministers and their translator sat down on the other. As always, they had tea served, and after a few minutes we were ready. I looked at Basanhu and nodded for him to make the introduction.

"My friends from America come to Mongolia as goodwill ambassadors of Jesus Christ," said Basanhu. The ministers were a little surprised, perhaps a little puzzled, but also looked interested and pleased, as if to say, "All right, the floor is yours. What do you have to say?"

The door seemed to be opened by their acceptance to this introduction and made me feel like I had made it to first base. It was important now, as it had been with the people in the ger when Jessica was given the lamb, to bond and connect with these men, and so once again I turned to history and said, "Back in the days of Genghis Khan, Mongolia was the most powerful nation in the world." Their eyebrows lifted and their eyes met mine. I was on their turf, and if I knew my subject well, we could be on common ground. "And one of the things that characterized the Mongolian Empire was that Genghis Khan granted religious freedom to the countries and peoples whom he conquered." The ministers smiled and nodded in agreement that this was true. We were on the same page. "Today the United States is the most powerful nation in the world and one of the foundations for which America is known, is that of religious freedom. Could it be that the God who created the world is pleased when a nation allows its people the freedom to choose how they will believe?"

I had no idea how much these men were wanting to hear the very things I was saying. After seventy years of Communist rule and being told, 'There is no God,' this very freedom was much on their hearts as well, now that they once again had an opportunity to be their own masters. They started talking, and their conversation was passionate and animated. I'd made it to second base.

The ministers began to talk of history, reliving the glory days of Mongolia, which of course they all knew but had not been free to talk about for seventy years. Stalin was so paranoid that he actually forbade the Mongols from talking about Genghis Khan. For Communists, it was like the whole world had begun in 1917, or so they wanted history to say. And so by coming to the Mongols boldly and yet in the humility of recognizing the greatness of their past, I had loosed something that had been bottled up for years and was longing to be released. The conversation that followed was exciting as we talked about freedom— part of the very image of God with which He created all people!

A half-hour later I said, "You know one of the things today in 1990, that President Bush looks for in extending the most favored nation status to trading partners is basic human rights, one of which is the freedom of religion." Then the ministers pulled out their copy of Senator Armstrong's letter and handed me back mine. And so we talked politics and trade and the goodwill of a state towards its people. The letter Senator Armstrong had written was outstanding, speaking of the Constitution and the foundation on which the United States had been established; it strongly urged the new Mongolian government to grant religious freedom to its people. Back and forth the conversation flowed and flowed. In my mind, I could see myself standing on third base and looking at home plate.

I glanced at my watch which said 12:55, and somehow I knew in five minutes it would all be over, so I reached in my pocket and pulled out a little book written by some men named Matthew, Mark, Peter, and John which had been translated into the Mongolian language by a Japanese translator. Standing up I said, "I would like to present you with a gift of the Holy Scriptures from the Christian Bible in the Mongolian language," and handed the booklet to the head minister with both hands and with a slight bow. The minister had also risen from his seat and was overwhelmed. How could this be? The Christian Scriptures in Mongolian? They eagerly began to look through the little booklet together. It was obvious that they were delighted, and so I reached inside my coat pocket and pulled out the other copy I had brought and said, "And would you please give this to the President of your country?" and handed the second booklet to him as well. It was a moment in the fullness of time, filled with sincerity and love, and the minister lifted up the book in one hand and the letter from Senator Armstrong in the other hand and said, "I will be glad to give these to the President of our country."

WILLIAM L. ARMSTRONG
COLORADO

United States Senate

WASHINGTON, DC 20510-0602

May 29, 1990

President Punsalmaagiin Ochibart
Mongolian People's Republic
Ulaanbaatar
Mongolia

Dear President Ochibart:

Congratulations to you and to the people of Mongolia for your brave progress toward democracy. We here in America rejoice to learn of the increase in individual liberty and personal freedom for Mongolia's citizens.

The cornerstone of American freedom and democracy has been our Constitution and its accompanying Bill of Rights. Our forefathers saw this document as fundamental to the effective rule of law, and so it has proven to be. As Americans, we congratulate Mongolia for its efforts to develop a Constitution that will serve your country as ours has served us -- as a foundation and guarantee of liberty and freedom.

Essential to our Constitution are its provisions which guarantee religious freedom. From the earliest days of the American colonies, men and women traveled to this new land to find freedom to express their religious beliefs as they desired. They saw the freedom to worship as they chose as a fundamental right of all mankind. The codification of this fundamental human right in the Constitution of the United States has been a key ingredient in the success of America's experiment in democracy. Without the right to choose one's own religion, no country can truly be called free.

As Mongolia continues its progress toward freedom and liberty, I urge you to make a concerted effort to guarantee all fundamental human rights, including the freedom of religion.

Best regards.

Sincerely

William L. Armstrong

WLA:cp

And so it was that the Lord fulfilled the vision that He had given to me for us to witness to the government leaders in Mongolia. I guess more than anything I felt that we had made some friends at the Ministry of Foreign Affairs. We had shown no fear and had been willing to come out in the open and be totally transparent. Our hearts were right. All we wanted to do was love these people with the love of the Lord and the Holy Spirit had done the rest. The presence of the Native Americans had been a key factor. How wonderfully the Lord was using these humble people who had been looked down upon for so many years. Surely we were witnessing a fulfillment of Jesus' words, "The first shall be last, and the last shall be first." God is faithful.

We shook hands, and the Mongolian ministers said again how very glad they were that we had come to their country and of course we felt the same. They invited us to come again another time and then escorted us down the stairs to the front door where we shook hands a final time, said our final goodbyes, and left.

Back at the hotel, we just had time for a quick lunch before heading off to the reception at the Peace and Friendship Association. Upon arriving, we were shown into a large room with long tables in a huge rectangle, which looked like they would seat around sixty people. It was great to see Ganbold, the director of the Peace and Friendship Association again, and I introduced him to Laura and the rest of our group. This was his second time to meet Native Americans, having met Milt Shirleson back in 1988. Ganbold and I were seated at the head table with Laura on my right and the rest of the team to both the left and the right. The room filled quickly with scholars and academic dignitaries, who were all keenly interested in the American Indians. Tea was served as always and we began to talk with those around us.

Finally Ganbold stood up, cleared his throat, and began the formal introductions. After he introduced me, I then introduced Ollie Heth,

Flint Poolaw, Jim Tohtsonie, Jim Lopez, Dr. Stanley Block, Starla Shetler, Laura and Jessica. Then each person around the room stood and introduced themselves, and we could see that we were among some of the elite of Mongolia's literary culture with poets, authors, historians, and scholars of various fields making up the Mongolian representation of the meeting.

We talked about the land bridge, and history, and the similarities that existed between Mongols and Native Americans. But coming off of the morning's events and all that had happened the last few days, it wasn't long before our group began to talk about the spiritual reasons that we had come to Mongolia. Naturally with these testimonies coming from the mouths of American Indians it had a profound affect upon all who were present. Ollie Heth from the Winnebago tribe spoke with great authority about the freedom there is in Christ for both men and women, and that in Christ we are all equal.

As this meeting was coming just three months after their democratic revolution, there was a zest for hearing new things and the conversation was lively and went on and on with many of the people around the room participating in the discussion. Dr. Block was there to help move the conversation along with his scholarly stature and manner of input, and of course with the very dynamic of the Native Americans' presence the dialogue grew ever more fascinating. The name of Jesus Christ was brought forth time and again, however it appeared that many of these learned men and women had never heard of Him. How amazing, considering this was the last decade of the twentieth century.

The official meeting lasted for a couple of hours and then we visited informally with the various Mongolian intellectuals and specialists wanting to talk further. If the length of time spent talking after the meeting was any indication, it was obvious we had made a good impression as we stayed on for another hour. Ganbold kindly helped us as a translator as well as Basanhu, and it was indeed an enjoyable time, exchanging a smile here, a handshake there, making as much eye contact as possible in an attempt to connect with these people and sow in the Spirit if only for a few moments. It was a pleasure to meet with all those who had come. Who knew, but perhaps there would come another time to water these seeds? A new day was dawning in Mongolia and there was no telling what might come next.

The excitement at the next meeting at Mongolian State University was equally dynamic as Dr. Block now lead our delegation. Along with college professors and other academics, members of the Chamber of Commerce were present, and various other branches of the business community. Once again, amidst the questions of culture, history, and anthropology, the reality of the Native American's faith and Dr. Block's faith in Jesus Christ were plainly presented.

The meeting lasted from 5 o'clock until 8 o'clock that evening and everyone arrived back at the hotel for a late dinner. Dr. Block seemed very pleased, as were the Native Americans. Our table talk was brisk as we enjoyed our dark bread and soup, salad with beef tongue, and the main course one last time! What an adventure we had been on! The Lord had answered the prayer that people had prayed for us from Eph. 6:19, and by His grace, we had opened our mouths and had spoken as we should.

Of all the principles in missions, one of the most important is that of bonding. In both the night in the ger where the old herdsman gave Jessica the lamb, and at the Ministry of Foreign Affairs, we used our knowledge about Mongolian culture and history to bond with the people. Our team bonded with the Mongols as we drank the fermented mare's milk of the Mongols and as we ate a meal with them in their traditional home. Finally, the fact that I knew their ancient word for God, and used it in telling about the incarnation of Christ, brought us into the Mongol's frame of reference, bonding us together with them, and helping them to understand that the God we were telling them about was the true God, the God of all peoples who had created the heavens and the earth.

The Old Herdsman

CHAPTER 5

Urbana and the JESUS Film

"I will also make you a light of the nations,
so that My salvation may reach to the ends of the earth."
Isaiah 49:6

The first missionaries to take up residence in Mongolia in seventy years now entered the country in late August, 1990. Twelve of them went through that winter of 1990-1991. (There were missionaries in Inner Mongolia of China in the '30s and '40s). Some of these people now came in as students to study the language, while others came in as English teachers. Everyone was still scrambling to catch up to the developments that had taken place in the course of world events in the last year. I had tried to make contact with some of these brothers and sisters before they left Hungary, where they had been studying Mongolian at a university in Budapest. But the phone line was poor and finally went dead. As a result, they had no knowledge of what had transpired on our trip and the changes that were taking place in Mongolia. And so they naturally came in wanting to keep a low profile, and just do their jobs or study the language. But I was sensing that it was a new day in Mongolia, the tide had turned, and the Mongols were wanting change. But more significant than any of this, God was opening the country.

A few months later at the close of 1990, the Urbana Mission Conference was held at the University of Illinois in Champaign, Illinois. With 19,000 plus in attendance, Urbana is Christendom's largest mission conference and is one of the most powerful events anywhere in the world. I had attended Urbana once before in 1987, but at that time in 1987, Mongolia was still a big unknown. Now at the close of 1990, the gospel had been preached and two men had been baptized.

The messages and speakers were superb and everyone greatly enjoyed this wonderful and amazing mission conference. The worship at the plenary sessions was dynamic, as 19,000 voices joined together to sing *Shine Jesus Shine*, and we enjoyed a mountain top experience. Equally dynamic was the whole display in the huge armory with hundreds of booths set up by different mission agencies, all pulsating with life. I had been given a corner of a booth and set up a board showing some of the pictures I'd taken in Mongolia.

On the last day of the conference, Dec. 31, 1990, about 2:30 p.m. I realized it was almost over and in just a few more hours the booths in the armory would be taken down, and we would proceed on toward the final communion service. All at once, I jumped up on the table at our booth, and shouted at the top of my voice, "MONGOLIA is OPEN! WHO will GO to MONGOLIA?" My voice split the air like a knife through the afternoon's drowsiness, and suddenly the entire armory came alive. In an instant, a man across the aisle who was an advocate for a ministry to Muslims, climbed quickly up a step ladder that was standing there, and gave out a Muslim call to prayer as loud as he could. The next thing we knew, we both had throngs of people wanting to hear more of what we had to say. They heard how the gospel was preached and received with great enthusiasm the past summer, and two men had been baptized in Mongolia for the first time in modern history.

An hour later I climbed up onto the table again and let go with another blast of the trumpet I believed the Lord was calling me to blow. "MONGOLIA is OPEN! WHO will GO to MONGOLIA?" Once more the call shattered the air from one end of the armory to the other, and more people gathered to hear the news of what had happened in

Mongolia. People all around me were smiling, and I knew I had done what the Lord had wanted. Years later, I was speaking at a church in Colorado and two elders came up and told how they had been there and remembered that day. And a few years after that, a mission executive who was the head of his denomination, and had been present that winter's afternoon, warmly recalled my petition. Little did I know how God would answer that call and the floodgates to Mongolia would come open. Within two years there would be over forty missionaries in Mongolia, with hundreds soon to follow, each proclaiming the amazing news that a man named Jesus Christ had risen from the dead.

A few months earlier in mid-September of 1990, I had called the JESUS film project to talk to them about putting the film into the Mongolian language. They were excited when I told them over the phone what had happened the preceding June, and flew me out to California to talk about what would need to be done to get the film dubbed into the Mongol language. I suggested that as we were dealing with a whole geo-political nation rather than just another language group, it would be best for Paul Eshleman, director of the JESUS Film project, to come to Mongolia to handle the negotiations. In Paul I found a kindred spirit for reaching the world for Christ, so we planned a trip into Mongolia together for January, 1991.

Paul would travel through Russia with two men and I through China with a man named Stottler Starr who had been praying for Mongolia for many years. Our flight arrived in Beijing and who should I see in the airport but Basanhu, my tour guide from the preceding summer. Basanhu had been invited to come to Washington and attend the National Prayer Breakfast. Incredible! We had but a couple of minutes together as his plane was due to leave momentarily as was mine. He told me things were going well, and that he wished he could be there to handle our negotiations, but that Mr. Boiyo would meet me at the airport and would arrange everything.

But then Stottler and I found out our baggage had not made the change of planes in San Francisco. "You go ahead," said Stottler, "you have people waiting for you. I'll stay behind and bring the baggage in a day or two." I was duly impressed with this humble man with the rather fanciful name of Stottler Starr.

Indeed Mr. Boiyo was there to meet me with a bear skin coat, praise God, which was just what I needed as all my warm clothing was in my lost luggage. He took me to the Ulaanbaatar Hotel where I met up with Paul and his traveling companions.

The next day at the Ministry of Foreign Affairs, we met with the same minister to whom I had given the Scriptures and the letter from Senator Armstrong the summer before. He was excited to see me and I was delighted to meet him again. We met in a beautiful, ornate receiving room where we took our customary tea. I introduced the minister to Paul Eshleman and the two friends of Paul's traveling with us, and then told him of our project. He was very pleased, and said he could provide us with a lawyer familiar with the legal arrangements that would need to be made with Mongol Kino (Films). I seemed to detect a spiritual hunger in this man. What had he heard? Or was it that he had read the little book containing Matthew, Mark, 1 Peter, and the Revelation of John? Something was different. It was as if the eternity in his heart had been awakened.

At Mongol Kino, Paul explained the project to their directors and asked if they could supply the actors, studio, etc. for the dubbing of the film. They said this was possible and that they would work together with the lawyer to draw up a contract.

As the head of the JESUS Film Project, Paul Eshleman had amazing stories to tell from deep in the heart of Africa, to a harrowing night in Beirut as it was under siege and being shelled. Mongolia would be the 186th language in which the film would be dubbed.

I asked Mr. Boiyo if he could get in touch with the director of the Mongolian Horse Association to see if we could try to find the old herdsman who had given Jessica the lamb the preceding summer. I said "try to find" because the Mongols who are living off the land in the countryside are still nomadic and will move two to three times in a year from summer to winter grazing areas, and they might not always be in the same location from one year to the next. I was learning that Mongols are a people who are ready to go at a moment's notice, and not having anything else to do in the middle of winter, the director of the horse association was eager to receive the request.

Mr. Boiyo lined up the only Toyota Land Cruiser in the country at the time to be at our disposal. This was the Zuulchin travel agency's number one car, used only for their most exclusive tourists, (usually big game hunters paying lots of money), and since this was the middle of January with no other tourists around, we got the Cruiser. It probably also helped to be in the movie business.

As we came to where the herdsman had been the summer before, nothing was there, the place was completely abandoned, and so we drove on and stopped at a small town ten kilometers miles down the road. The horse association director made some enquires and came back smiling. The old herdsman was just over the hill, well a few hills, well actually thirty-five kilometers (twenty miles) off the main road and over several hills. But the ground was hard and the snow not too deep, so we should have no problem finding him.

We all gained a pretty keen insight into Mongolia that day traveling cross-country, over hill and dale through the frozen Mongolian countryside. A couple of times we stopped at gers to ask directions, and the people wanted us to just stay right there, spend the day, and drink some tea. Why go any further? But I was determined to find the old herdsman, so we pressed on. We finally crossed over a hill that gave a magnificent panorama of the countryside that few people from the West have ever seen. The expansiveness was breathtaking, but to the Mongol people who lived there in their gers, it was just home. All the same they too appreciate the beauty of their homeland and love it dearly.

One of the outstanding distinctions of Mongolia is the absence of fences. It was quite a revelation to realize there were essentially no fences from where we were standing in Mongolia, all the way through Kazakhstan to the Caspian Sea, right through the heart of Central Asia. It didn't take much imagination to transcend time and know we were seeing the same Mongolia that the famous monk Abby Huc had also seen in the time of the Great Khans when he traveled there in the mid-thirteenth century. How long had the Mongols inhabited this land?

The Great Wall of China was built roughly 450 B.C. by the Chin dynasty from which the country and the people derive their name. The reason the wall was built was to keep the wild barbarians (Mongols) from the north from invading. The Mongols were nomadic with no appreciation for the finer things of sedentary Chinese culture. They would ride down from the steppe and raid, take whatever they wanted from the Chinese, and ride back again with no one being too eager to pursue them. It could be called a clash of worldviews. How long this went on, no one really knows, but finally the Emperor Chin evidently had enough and decided to build a wall, a GREAT WALL to keep the Mongols out... which it did until the thirteenth century.

On my first visit to the Great Wall in 1988, I remember standing there totally overwhelmed as most people are when they see the Wall for the first time. It is truly incredible, and as I stood there talking to myself, I said, "How did Genghis Khan make it over this wall?"

"He bribed the Chinese on the other side," came a voice from behind that startled me out of my daydream. I turned and there was an Englishman with his pipe and hat who could easily have passed for a

Stottler Starr

don at any university in Britain.

So I asked, "What do you mean?" And the distinguished looking gentleman continued, "After many months of his army being stalled on the northern side, unable to breach the wall militarily, Chinggis Khan finally had to bribe a Chinese gatekeeper. And that, was how he got through, to the demise of the Chinese." It was the first time I had ever heard Genghis called Chinggis, but the professorial Englishman stood quite confidently, assuring me that he knew what he was talking about and was giving me the correct story, which the average tourist would never know. (I later learned he was right on all accounts.) Also, the name Genghis is actually pronounced Chinggis by the Mongols. How this became spelled and pronounced Genghis in English, I have no idea. He smiled and knocked the ashes from his pipe and moved on up the wall.

At last we came to the herdsman's winter camp. It was on the side of a hill and had a view of some thirty miles or more to the west in the foreground, and further mountains showing on the horizon a hundred miles or so in the distance. Stottler Starr had now joined us from Beijing with our luggage, and as he looked out over the frozen landscape he was experiencing something of a fulfillment of a dream. The Mongols brought a horse over and Stottler got on and rode around.

I asked about Jessica's lamb, and a few minutes later one of the young Mongol children came holding the lamb, now seven months old and a good deal bigger. We ate a meal together and I told how these men who had come with me were also believers in Jesus Christ. After dinner

I picked up an old guitar that was in the ger and started to play a song I'd written called "The Great Horned Owl". When I came to the part where I actually hoot like an owl, it must have sounded like the real thing because a cat that was asleep in the ger jumped about three feet in the air and let out a shriek of sheer terror, sure that its end had come. Well that stopped the song cold as we laughed until the tears ran down our cheeks, Mongols and Americans alike.

Never to be outdone in singing, the herdsman's wife then stood to her feet to sing one of the famous Mongolian "long songs". Once again we were on the inside of this amazing culture. The "long song" is pensive and penetrating, a style that is not found anywhere else in the world, quite a distinct sound coming forth in long mournful trills and slides, jumping octaves suddenly from the roof of the mouth to the back of the throat, that are uniquely Mongolian. The weather was bitterly cold outside, but it was warm and the atmosphere rich inside. We drank milk tea as it was not the season for fermented mare's milk. Then to our surprise when it was time to go, the old herdsman who had given Jessica the lamb, whose name was Luump, jumped in the car and rode into town with us. He probably reasoned that it was not everyday that the fanciest car in all of Mongolia drives into your front yard, and he might as well take advantage of it. At the edge of Ulaanbaatar he called to the driver of the Land Crusier to stop. He jumped out, said a simple goodbye, and was gone into the night. Mongols. What a different people!

The next day we signed the contract with Mongol Kino, which they had drawn up while we had taken our outing the day before. They would supply us with the studio, technical equipment, and actors to do the dubbing for a price that was reasonable. Everything had gone smoothly.

That night Mr. Boiyo hosted a little ceremony in celebration and invited Boldbaatar to join us. Bold, as we called him, had been diligently studying English with a couple of the missionaries who were now in the country and was speaking quite well after only five months of study. Mr. Boiyo had set a small American flag and a Mongolian flag on the table side-by-side, and provided a cake as well. Mr. Boiyo made a little speech, and Paul Eshleman made a speech, and we drank a toast with soda to all that God was doing in Mongolia. It was so obvious that we were witnessing the Lord at work, opening up the country. And so we came to understand a little more that evening that the missionary enterprise is really God's. He is the one moving it and driving it onward as it is written of the Messiah in Isaiah 49:6, "It is too small a thing that you should be my servant to raise up the tribes of Israel, I will also make you a light of the nations, so that My salvation may reach to the ends of the earth." And there we were.

CHAPTER 6

Signs, Wonders, & a Church is Born.

"I say to you that I will build My church,
and the gates of hell will not prevail against it."
Matthew 16:18

When I arrived home, a man named Dick Hochreiter called and asked about us going into Mongolia together. Dick had been to Mongolia once, but without much success. So we arranged a trip for mid-April. I had two other men who also wanted to go to Mongolia, and Dick had three who wanted to go with him, so this would make a team of seven.

As we met at the airport in San Francisco we formed a little huddle and I asked the question, "What's our job? What are we going to do? The Bible says that 'God is love,' and as the Great Commandment says that we are to love the Lord with all of our heart and to love our neighbor as ourselves, we can safely say that we have a mandate from God to go over there and love these people. Love never fails." Everyone agreed. Everyone smiled. We were one. And with that in our minds and in our hearts we boarded the plane headed for China and then on to Mongolia. What would God do?

Basanhu made sure that he was assigned to be our tour guide and Mr. Boiyo and Boldbaatar were also there to meet our plane. When we arrived at the Ulaanbaatar Hotel, we were spotted by two young newspaper reporters looking for interviews, and they made a beeline for our group as we entered the lobby. It was now mid-April 1991, and the country had been free for a year. The young reporters were eager for news from abroad.

Upstairs in my room, the two reporters sat down and opened up with the same question that was asked to Milt Shirleson, the Navajo Indian, three years before. "Why have you come to our country?"

"We have come to Mongolia because God loves the Mongol people." I said. I then went over the same story of the incarnation I had told Mr. Boiyo in 1988, and to the people in the ger the year before in 1990, that the true God was a God of love, and that He had become a man, and that man's name was Jesus Christ and that He had done . . . This was not exactly what the reporters were expecting but they took notes, and reported the story accurately the next day in the state-run newspaper.

The next morning at breakfast Basanhu told us that we had been invited to teach English in the Mongolian State Teacher's College. We all looked at one another and in a moment realized this was the platform the Lord was giving us. So off we went without a thought to the fact that there wasn't an English teacher in our group.

There were about fifteen students in the room that morning as we were introduced as guest teachers from America. Hmm. English. Right. "Okay, 'A,' A is for Adam. Adam was the first man who ever lived on the earth." And so we began our lesson in English. Our job as we understood it was to love people and if this was the venue that the Lord was providing then this was the venue we were to use. And it soon became apparent that the students were not so much interested at that time in English as they were interested in us. And so by following the leading of the Lord, even though it was into an unexpected arena, we suddenly found ourselves before a group of people who simply wanted to hear whatever we had to say.

One of the members of our team was a worship leader at his home church who had brought along his guitar. And so the Mongol students wanted us to sing to them, which we were glad to do. But as we began to sing it became noticeable that we were not just singing songs but that something else was happening. We were worshipping God.

It wasn't too long before the door peeped open and a teacher from down the hall motioned for the teacher of our class to come to the door. After a brief explanation from our teacher as to who we were, the other teacher said, "When they finish teaching your class, could they come and teach my class too?" And so the Lord began to spontaneously open doors for the next two weeks, and like Jesus and his disciples, sometimes we hardly had time to eat.

Our English classes continued throughout the week as did some evening classes we volunteered to hold, and on Saturday the students wanted to take us on an outing to a famous resort outside of Ulaanbaatar called Terelj, a couple of hours away. By then the numbers attending our English classes and other meetings had reached about forty. Much of the week had been spent bonding and making friends, but on the outing we began to share more of the gospel and invited the students to come to a service the next day.

One of the members of our team was a pastor named Dennis Potter. Dennis was an excellent preacher and storyteller. That Sunday morning after his message, Dennis asked if anyone there was sick, and one girl raised her hand. "Ask her to come here," Dennis said, and the girl came forward.

"What is the problem?" Dennis asked, and the girl who appeared to be in her mid-twenties said there was something wrong with her stomach. Dennis began to teach saying, "The Lord Jesus told us that we were to lay hands upon the sick and pray for them and that the sick person would recover." As he gently laid his hand upon the girl's forehead, she was overcome by the power of God and fainted, and the whole room was astir.

"Tell the people not to be afraid," Dennis said to Basanhu who was translating, "this is simply the power of God healing the girl", and he began to teach them the word of the Lord about healing. Seven or eight minutes later the girl woke up and getting to her feet, she looked bewildered but had a smile on her face. We asked her how she felt and she said the pain in her stomach was gone. Everyone was astounded. "Is there anybody else here who is sick?" asked Dennis, and amazingly enough two young men came forward, though a little hesitantly as might be expected. The next thing anybody knew Dennis had laid his hands on them in the name of the Jesus and they too were now lying on the floor. Everyone in the room was excited, not unlike the stories we read about in the gospels where Jesus is healing people.

And so it was that the Lord began to move in power among the Mongols. By the end of the following week at one meeting people were lined up and when Dennis touched a young girl on the forehead, two people at the other end of the line fell over. It was amazing and beyond anyone's ability to predict or control.

As we went into the second week, it seemed like we needed to draw things to some kind of a conclusion before we left, and so we decided that we would hold a baptism on the following Sunday afternoon. There were now twenty missionaries in Mongolia and some of them had begun to attend our evening meetings, which were held in a classroom at a local elementary school.

On Monday night we announced that we would be having a baptism the next Sunday before we left, so if anyone who had received Christ wanted to be baptized, they needed to come to a special baptism class on Wednesday night. When we came together again two days later the room was packed and so we began to teach on baptism. We went over the Great Commission, the story of the Ethiopian eunuch, and Romans 6, but we felt like there was still more that needed to be covered so we said, "If you want to be baptized on Sunday, you need to come to baptism class again tomorrow night."

The baptism class on Thursday night was again filled with the people who had started to attend the meetings no matter where they were being held. And so besides teaching on baptism, we preached the gospel, shared the love of God, and ministered to the people's needs in Jesus' name. We announced that on Sunday morning there would be a worship service and that all were invited, and to bring their friends. That Sunday morning we decided Boldbaatar should do some of the preaching as he was beginning to show signs of being a good Bible teacher. And sure enough Bold gave an impassioned message to which people responded.

Throughout the two weeks we had been in the country, the Lord had added to the number of believers almost daily. Though the numbers were not like what Peter experienced in Acts 2 and 3, the dynamic was similar. If you take into account that before meeting us that week, these Mongols with whom we were now coming in contact had never heard of Jesus Christ, had no background knowledge about the one true God, had never heard of the Ten Commandments or anything else concerning the Bible, it becomes obvious the Lord was moving with power, and the people could see this.

We had no idea how many people might actually come forward to be baptized that afternoon. It is one thing to attend a meeting, but quite another to make a public proclamation by way of baptism. However it was obvious that many of the forty to sixty people who had been attending the meetings had met the Lord as they testified how the Lord had touched them, and that they felt as if they were a new person. And so there was much to praise the Lord for, but we had no idea how many would come forward to be baptized. At that time there was only Basanhu, Mr. Boiyo, and Boldbaatar in all of Mongolia who were baptized. What would happen that afternoon?

As we came down the stairs at the hotel to go to the baptism, two Americans were waiting for us in the lobby. As they approached us one of them said, "Are you the people who are going to hold a baptism this afternoon?" I nodded yes. "We are with the Associated Press and wherever we go in this city, people are talking about you. Would it be all right with you if we came to this baptism?"

"Come along," I said with a sense of wonder at how the Lord was putting things together, and out the door we went.

The baptism was to be held at an indoor swimming pool and people were already waiting outside the building when we arrived. We went inside and into a dressing room, and when we came out, the pool area was completely surrounded by more than seventy people who had come to witness the baptism. Besides the American journalists, there were the two Mongolian newspapermen who had interviewed us two weeks before when we had arrived at the hotel. There was also one big Mongolian cameraman with a video camera, and many other people who had brought cameras as well. A dozen resident missionaries were in attendance with big smiles on their faces.

The air was electric. Nothing like this had ever happened in Mongolia. The presence of the Holy Spirit was just as it had been that night in the herdsman's ger the year before. God was with us. Great joy was on people's faces as we began a time of praise and worship, singing the simple choruses we had taught these very first Mongol believers, and we all began to sing in Mongolian, "Holy, holy, holy Lord… God of power and might… heaven and earth are filled with your glory," and so we sang and worshipped the Lord. God was opening up Mongolia. This was his doing as he was fulfilling the promise he had made to Abraham, that in the One who would come through him, "all the families of the earth would be blessed."

I shared a short message explaining for all those who were present the new birth in Christ, and the meaning and significance of baptism. Dick was beaming as he stepped into the pool with Boldbataar, and then one by one, Mongol after Mongol entered the water. I was so caught up in the euphoria of the moment that I forgot to count and had no idea how many people had been baptized. But fortunately Mr. Boiyo was at the end of the pool with pencil and paper and carefully counted thirty-four people who were baptized. The Associated Press took pictures like there would be no tomorrow and their story appeared in a Minneapolis newspaper a week later. We sang, we shouted, we hugged our new brothers and sisters in Christ. We enjoyed the presence of the Holy Spirit in a momentous way that will never be forgotten by all those who were there. It was April 28, 1991.

As I entered the dressing room after the baptism there was Dennis Potter in the center of a circle of people with his hand on someone's head praying for them. Already on the floor were two other people for whom he had prayed. It seemed the Holy Spirit didn't want to stop. Evidently the news of the healings that had taken place throughout the week had spread, for when we returned to the hotel there were people from thirty miles away waiting for us in the lobby wanting to be prayed for. In Mark 3:8 it says that, "a great multitude heard of all that Jesus was doing and came to Him," and so it was in this case.

Something was now taking place in Mongolia that had never happened before– something wonderful, something beautiful, something eternal– a church was being born. And there was no doubt that it was the planting of the Lord. We had come to Mongolia with right priorities, to love people as the Lord calls his people to do, and as a result we had seen him move in a most dramatic way. Doors had opened spontaneously. News traveled by word of mouth in such a fashion that even the Associated Press, there for completely different reasons, had heard about what was going on. People were being saved and healed and the living God was being worshipped in spirit and in truth. Jesus had begun raising up a people to be called by His name in this far off corner of the earth.

CHAPTER 7

Communion

"But let a man examine himself,
and so let him eat of the bread and drink the cup."
1 Corinthians 11:28

A couple of months later in June of 1991, I brought a team of seven people to Mongolia to study language and culture for the summer. From the thirty-four who were baptized in April, the church began growing in that summer of 1991, and by August had become more than seventy people. A young scholar and doctor of veterinary medicine named Dash, who would one day become the director of the Mongolian Union Bible Society, was one of the thirty-four people baptized back in April, and together with Basanhu and Boldbaatar, the three of them now formed the leadership of what was called the Fellowship Church. Bold and Dash were the teachers along with various missionaries and they taught from the Mongolian New Testament.

Our last Sunday before we were to leave, Basanhu came up to me at the end of the service and asked if I would lead them in Communion. The new church was only a few months old and with all that was going on had yet to hold Communion, so it was a good opportunity to teach them what Communion was all about.

"We have been telling you that Christianity is not a religion but a relationship with God, our Father, and His Son Jesus Christ. But also our relationship is with each other. And because we are all human we sometimes fail to do or say the things we should to one another. But as we see written in the Bible, in 1 Corinthians 11, you need to look on page 553 in your books at 1 Cor. 11:23-27..." Most of the Mongols at this time had obviously never heard of the book of Corinthians so I would take time to make sure we were all reading the same passage and then I would tell them who the Corinthians were, and that this was a letter written to the church that had been started in the city of Corinth, by a man named Paul, and then explain who Paul was, etc.

"We read here in Corinthians that when we take Communion we must not do so in an unworthy manner, but as the body of Christ we need to make our relationships right with one another. So all the people who have been baptized should come up front." About thirty people began to rise from their seats to make their way forward. We were meeting in a small theater at the time with a stage, and so as all the baptized believers came up onto the stage about twenty to twenty-five people were left watching.

When all the people who were going to take communion had come to the front I went over the instructions about forgiving one another once again, and finally asked, "Now does everybody understand?" They all nodded assent and so I said, "Well what we are going to do now is

The church had grown to around 70

just wait here a minute and if anyone has something they need to apologize to someone else about, you need to do that now."

And so we stood and a couple of minutes passed with no one moving when suddenly another missionary, Al Gentleman, walked over to me. I thought Al was going to say something like, 'I don't think they understand,' but instead he put his arms around me and started to weep, saying he had been angry with me that week and would I forgive him? I embraced Al and said, "Of course I forgive you," and the joy of the Lord was evident in our renewed faces. It was then that the Mongols understood what the Lord's Supper was all about, and one by one they began to cross the stage to make a relationship right with a brother or a sister. And so we held the church's first Communion service.

After we had partaken of the bread and the cup and everybody made their way back to their seats, I thought that the service would be over. Wrong. It was just beginning, as one person after another person who had watched the Communion service began to rise to their feet and testify as to what they had just witnessed. "Now we see that this Christianity is not just a bunch of words but is indeed powerful and practical to our lives." On and on they went for over half an hour talking about the things they had seen that day, and what it meant to them.

And that's the way it should be when Christianity is lived out before the world. Our faith needs to be alive, it must be active, it must be real, there must be something to it. And when our faith is lived out in spirit and in truth, even the unbelievers will testify that God is surely in our midst.

In July our team went into the countryside to witness the famous *Naadam* celebration, which is comprised of what the Mongols call "the three manly sports" of wrestling, archery, and horseracing. All three are quite unique. The archery is interesting as old men draw handmade long bows, and aim at an oblong target about a hundred yards away. Women shoot from about seventy-five yards.

Wrestling is the number one spectator sport in Mongolia as it takes place year-round, is filled with great pomp and pageantry, and is quite distinct from wrestling in other countries. In preparation to meet their opponent, the wrestlers flap their arms like eagles' wings, and then slap their thighs, as if to say "I'm gonna kick your..."

But it is the horserace that makes *Naadam* one of the most spectacular sporting events in the world, and is the love of the country. The race itself is thirty kilometers long, cross-country over the hills. But the outstanding feature is that the riders are children, ages four to eleven! Children riding a galloping horse for thirty kilometers (eighteen miles) and there may be as many as three hundred to six hundred horses and riders in one race!

At the finish line, the families gather on foot or horseback, three deep for a quarter of a mile, waiting for the children to arrive. It is quite something to see 5,000 people on horseback at one time in one place. What power the ancient Mongols must have felt as they marched out in the hey-day of the Khan's armies with 100,000 men on horseback. Even so, 5,000 people on horses was impressive, and you needed to watch yourself or get run over.

And then someone with binoculars cries out, 'More irlee!' (the horses are coming), and everyone immediately repeats the call, and the excitement really begins to build. Off in the distance, barely specks in a cloud of dust, the dark shapes of horses and riders still two to three miles off can be seen. The people began to jockey along the finish line for a better vantage point from which to see the race. If you were on foot, you really had to watch out for getting stepped on by a horse.

The racers had become strung out over several miles as would be expected over the course of thirty kilometers with three hundred to six hundred entries. Now with the first riders still a quarter of a mile off, the crowd picked up the yell, heee-ya, heee-ya, and the front runners slapped their horses with their leather and wood quirts. The children's faces beamed as they crossed the finish line and their families on horseback broke ranks from the crowd and rushed down to sweep up their sons and daughters in a wild family jubilee. The next thing we knew, there was a kind of dance going on with 5,000 people on horseback, riding around this way and that, as the whole hillside came alive with people riding every which way. Our team, which included Mike McKay who would eventually marry a Mongol woman and stay in Mongolia, could only look at each other, laugh, and say, 'Wow.' There was nothing else like this in the world!

After the Urbana mission conference in 1990, where I had stood up on the table to proclaim that Mongolia was open, I became acquainted with an organization called Chief which was located in Phoenix. Chief is the largest Indian Mission organization in the world run by Tom and Huron Clause. So I started talking to Tom and his son Huron, about the idea of sending American Indians to Mongolia. They greatly liked the idea and said that they themselves would like to go to Mongolia.

Tom and Huron arrived in Mongolia in August of 1991, just after our summer team had returned home. Basanhu and the Fellowship Church readily welcomed Tom and Huron, and once again that interesting dynamic between Mongols and Native Americans began to take effect and they quickly and easily spoke of spiritual things on a deep level. Here the teaching gift that the Native Americans possess was well utilized. They spoke and taught extensively and with great authority in the fledgling church. They thoroughly enjoyed the time they spent with their distant relatives the week they were in Mongolia. Then just before leaving they too took a trip down to see the famous Gobi Desert. As Indians of the southwestern U.S. they could readily identify with the life of the Mongols living in the Gobi.

As Tom and Huron came back to Phoenix we scheduled a Saturday breakfast to get together and talk about their trip. Tom had some interesting insights, and both he and Huron confirmed that there was a definite link between Native Americans and Mongols. They had had a wonderful trip and brought back some excellent pictures from their time in Mongolia. And so the time seemed ripe to tell Tom and Huron what was on my heart.

"You know guys, I've got something I want to share with you. I feel that as a white man I have too much cultural baggage to try and beat this drum to mobilize Native Americans to go to Mongolia like I am trying to do," and they nodded their heads understandingly. "And so it seems to me, now that you have been to Mongolia yourselves, with all of your contacts from Alaska to Peru, that you're in a much better position to bring this vision to Native Americans than I am," and naturally they agreed. They also went on to say they thought this was something that Native peoples needed to hear and that they would talk about it as they circulated and taught among the Native American tribes.

It was with mixed feelings that I left the restaurant that Saturday morning. The news of my taking Native Americans into Mongolia had spread throughout much of the missions world, being talked about at places like the Fuller School of World Missions as well as Columbia and Trinity Seminaries. But I knew, as did Tom and Huron, that what I had said was true. And so, having sown the vision among Native Americans that God wanted to also use them in world missions, I felt the Lord saying it was time that I let go of this aspect of reaching Mongolia. It was time to move on.

CHAPTER 8

The Premiere

"That they may all be one; even as You, Father, are in Me,
and I in You, that they also may be in Us,
so that the world may believe that You sent Me."
John 17:21

Things were now moving swiftly towards the premiere of the JESUS
film. I was able to contact and invite Christian recording artist Randy Stonehill to come to Mongolia for a series of concerts to help draw the
attention of the young people to the film. The premiere was set for January 11, 1992, and Randy's first concert was January 8. With the temperature at minus thirty degrees Farenheit, this was a little cool for a Southern
California rock and roll star. When we arrived in the country, Ganbold,
who had arranged the hall for the concerts, had also pulled together the
best musicians in Mongolia to accompany Randy. ALL Randy had to do
was teach them his songs . . . and weld them into a band . . . in three days
. . . and all through an interpreter! I thought Randy might balk at this, but
he was game, and began to work with the musicians to get them ready.

The small concert hall began to fill on opening night and slowly all
two hundred seats were occupied. Randy is a genuine professional and
great showman and handled the cross-cultural dimension of the evening
quite well as we had his songs translated for the audience.

It was the somewhat unreliable technology in Mongolia that presented the biggest problem as on opening night halfway through Randy's first set, right in the middle of his song, the lights went out. But, miraculously, before he could miss a beat, someone in the middle of the auditorium hit Randy with the beam of a huge flashlight, and then several other flashlights joined the first, and the show carried on. For Mongols having the lights go out was just business as usual and they were the ones who had brought the flashlights. What a lifesaver. Then I suppose an angel overcame a demon in the heavenlies and the lights came back on a half-hour later and Randy was able to finish the show and put in a plug in for everyone to be sure and go see this movie called JESUS.

A businessmen and professional delegation had come in from South Dakota including one state senator, to be part of the premiere and they began to mix and talk with the Mongolian Parliament members. Some were experts in industry and they met with their Mongolian counterparts. Some were lawyers and they met with Mongol lawyers, bankers with bankers, American forestry experts with Mongolian forestry experts, etc. All these had come in several days prior to the premiere and invited their Mongolian peers to attend the premiere of the film. As a result nearly the entire four hundred and fifty member Parliament attended the opening of the JESUS film!

When Randy and I and our party arrived at the theater, the packed house of a thousand people in the largest theater in Mongolia was an incredible sight to see. The South Dakota delegation had done their job well, as had Randy, as had the English teachers and various other missionaries living in the country. Seats had been saved for us and we began to make our way through the audience.

Excitement filled the air. Paul Eshleman had flown in the night before along with some important dignitaries whom I was told would be speaking at the opening ceremony. A few minutes later, who should lead the speakers out onto the stage but Basanhu, accompanied by an athletic looking man, a man in uniform, another man, and Paul Eshleman. The proceedings began.

The other man was Craig Lawrence who was the leader of the South Dakota delegation that had done such a wonderful job connecting with Mongolian professionals the last few days and expressed his hope for future partnership between Americans and Mongolians. The athlete turned out to be the Olympic gold medal winner in wrestling, John Peterson, and the man in uniform was introduced as a United States general. Each one spoke for a minute with Basanhu translating and then Paul Eshleman said let the show begin. In the next six years the JESUS film would be shown over four thousand times in almost every city, town, and village across the country. The JESUS film had come to Mongolia and would be greatly used by God.

CHAPTER 9

The Church Explodes

"And the Lord was adding to their number day by day,
those who were being saved."
Acts 2:47

After the premier, our family moved to Mongolia in 1992 to help with the harvest. Over and over again, in any church you would attend on a Sunday morning, you would hear Mongols giving testimony of either having met Jesus in the past week, or having led someone to Christ. From that day on these new believers, young and old alike, would sing and sing and sing, praising and worshipping the Lord. They had tremendous zeal. Foreigners would come to Mongolia on short-term mission trips, and return home in absolute amazement at what they had seen going on in this far off land.

One of the biggest challenges for missionaries is to recognize and overcome their own ethnocentrism, and to realize the people whom they are trying to reach are also ethnocentric. Therefore, allowances must be made for the others' ethnocentrism, if one is to communicate effectively. The bottom line is to understand that one culture is not necessarily better than another, but simply different.

But whether or not the things being said were always clearly understood, the Mongols were experiencing something they had never known before. They were coming to know love in a new way. The people who had come to

Mongolia in the name of the Lord, had to come to love, and the spirit, attitude, and acts of love are not necessarily communicated through words, but through care, concern, accessibility and availability, and this was the kind of people whom the Lord had brought to Mongolia when the churches were just starting. They came to give, and they came to love.

New workers Dave & Kerry Miller with Rick, Laura, & Jessica

In particular in those years from 1991 to 1995, a lot of the impetus for growth in the church was a result of short-term workers, many of them teachers who had come to Mongolia for a year or two, to teach English. Those teachers loved their students and the students knew it. And as the word of God says, "Love never fails."

Often the students would be invited to a church service in order to hear English spoken by a native speaker. But what was being said in English, was also being translated into Mongolian, and so what the young people ended up hearing in their own language was the remarkable story about a man named Jesus who had risen from the dead.

Sometimes the meetings were so packed that the young people would be standing in the hall outside the door. Many young Mongols inside were sitting two to a seat, with the aisles equally filled with people sitting bunched together, as they came to listen.

One day a Swedish missionary was leading the meeting, and with arms outstretched in an expression of openness and dependence on God, his head back and looking up to receive from God whatever the Lord would give that day, and the room was absolutely silent. We were on holy ground. We could barely hear the almost whispered prayer coming from the missionary, but mostly, it seemed like we were experiencing something similar to Genesis 1, as the Spirit of God was hovering over the room, pregnant with life, wanting to give birth, touching these young Mongols who had never experienced anything like this before.

The silence lingered and the moments were precious. Finally the young Swedish missionary prayed out loud and the prayer was translated. Many of these young Mongols had never heard or seen prayer done in this fashion. He then began to teach and the subject was, appropriately, the love of God expressed through His Son who had died on a cross to forgive the sins of the world. The young people were enthralled and you could almost see the word of forgiveness going into them like water into a dry sponge, only this water was alive.

After an hour of teaching, the praise of Jesus began again, and the young people would stay and sing and sing and sing, at least for another hour, maybe two. Time was not of the essence. The wonder and process of regeneration was the order of the day. And so it continued throughout the fall of 1992. Wednesday and Sunday meetings were filled with hundreds of young people. Significant progress had been made that year. The number of people attending the churches grew from two hundred to over a thousand! One church had mushroomed from a Bible study of seven to over three hundred and eighty people in only ten months.

New believers just a few weeks old in the Lord might be on their way to a Bible study and come across an old friend whom they would simply sweep along with them to the meeting. Afterwards they would all go out and get drunk. Remember these were very new believers, just a few weeks old, still drinking, still smoking, etc. They were not most churches' ideal candidates to do evangelistic outreach. But these new believers had encountered the living Christ, and had been born again. They had been forgiven and they had a story to tell. Changes were taking place in their lives and they knew it. Within a short time through steady discipleship their old bad habits fell away. Soon these same young people would get married, have children, become sound in doctrine, lead churches and live exemplary lives. The Holy Spirit was moving in a most remarkable way.

And so the lives of the Mongol believers became testimonies unto God as they experienced the beauty and absolute wonderful reality of people being born again in Jesus Christ. As the Scriptures say, "All who believed Him, and received Him, He gave the right to become the children of God. They are reborn. This is not a physical birth resulting from human passion or plan. This rebirth comes from God."

Though foreign mission agencies were certainly at work and doing all they could, it was the Mongols who now began to lead the way in evangelizing their people. Our family had an entire set of videos of animated stories of the New Testament, which were superbly done, and soon the Mongol believers were asking if they could borrow them. A video player could be a powerful tool, and so we loaned out our videos and the TV with its built in video player. Often we sent this useful little 13" TV/VCR, to small towns with outreach teams so that people could watch the JESUS film. A ger might be packed with thirty people watching the movie. So the missionaries would supply a few tools, such as a TV/VCR, and the Mongol church members would gladly and zealously accept the responsibility of bringing the message of salvation to their people. And the Mongols turned out to be born evangelists. As far as evangelism went, the job of the missionaries was becoming more and more to encourage and give the Mongols a few hints along the way. The missionaries were giving guidance, but the gospel was exploding in Mongolia through the testimony of the Mongolian believers themselves.

"The gospel in Mongolia is spread by a cup of *suutei tsai*" became a well known saying among the Mongols. The most common thing in Mongolia was their everyday drinking of milk tea, and the believers easily understood this as the most natural way they could witness to their countrymen. Whether Mongols lived in the countryside or in the city, everyone drinks milk tea. So Mongols all across the country drank their *suutei tsai* and listened to the amazing news that a man named Jesus Christ had risen from the dead!

A key feature of the emerging Mongol churches were the '*gering* groups' (home groups). The meetings would begin with tea and fellowship as Mongol culture and protocol would expect. Then songs were sung, and the word of God was taught. In the first group I led, we began with Genesis. "Verse one says that God created the world. Now what do we know about people who create things, such as artists and musicians? They feel things deeply. This is what God is like. He feels things deeply, for the character and the very nature of God is love. The creation of the world is the expression of God Himself. His desire now is to bring people around the world into a relationship with Himself."

A few weeks later a young man got up at the close of the lesson and put on his coat to leave, instead of hanging around like the others. I quickly grabbed the translator, moved to the door and caught him just as he was going out. "Where are you going?" I asked.

"To preach the gospel and start churches," was his reply and out the door he went. I didn't know if my teaching had been good or bad, but that young man was true to his word, and taking Jesus at his word, set out like the apostles in Matthew 10, taking nothing for his journey. His name was Arinbold and he set out in dependence upon the Lord, believing that the laborer was worthy of his meat, as the Scriptures said. He was gone five months right through the dead of winter and his journey took him all the way to the far western region of Mongolia! Mongols are a very amazing people. Six years later when the Mongolian Evangelical Alliance was formed, he would be their first executive director.

The three largest churches that emerged at this time were Urden Gegee, Muheen Xair, and Hope Church. Urden Gegee was the largest at that time and grew to over five hundred people. They held services twice each week with wonderful singing and preaching. Skits and dramas also began to play a major part in Mongols communicating the gospel to one another. It seemed the church was blessed with an abundance of talent. With singing being so much a part of Mongol's lives, it was only natural that choirs would emerge and Urden Gegee was the first church to have a real choir. The church had been started by a Korean missionary named Hwang. This man was gifted in training leaders

One of the early baptisms

and was responsible for many Mongols who would go forth into the ministry and start other churches.

Baptisms are always one of the greatest experiences for any church. In Mongolia these would often take place out of doors down on the banks of the Tol River amidst joyful singing.

But what all was going on in the lives of these young Mongols who were coming into a relationship with God? Some had struggles in the home and experienced rejection. But just as often, the parents of the young people who were getting saved saw such a dramatic change come into their children's lives that they changed from being antagonistic to tolerant, and then to supportive. Their children who had become Christians were no longer getting drunk. They weren't running around with questionable people. They weren't telling lies. About the biggest problem they had with their young Christian children was that they were constantly going to meetings.

Possibly as much as anything these new Mongol believers were beginning to catch a little hope for their lives. The new birth that was taking place within them was producing a zeal that was truly remarkable. Yes, many stumbled along the way, however that happens to people everywhere. These Mongols who had come to Christ had now tasted something better than their old life offered, something bigger than themselves which they had never known before. They had now entered the kingdom of God and tasted eternal life.

Muheen Xair was another church that had a Korean leader. Young Choon Lee was a loving pastor and as a consequence his church began to grow. Starting churches is not always easy but he and his team persevered through the difficult times until the breakthrough came. Soon there were thirty people, then forty, fifty, and it just kept growing. At the end of 1995, the church had a Christmas party and over two hundred people attended. The party lasted for five hours with skits, songs, nativity reenactments, testimonies, and lots of food. It was great. Unsaved family members who attended the celebration at the invitation of their believing relatives were most favorably impressed with what they saw and heard that day. Mongolians were really experiencing the wonderful fellowship of the Spirit that Jesus gives.

A year later the church had rented an old theater for its Sunday morning services. Young Choon was standing in the back one Sunday morning during the worship service while the young people were leading in singing some choruses. "Look at this," I said to him and pointed out the ones in the congregation who were following along with the hand motions accompanying the songs. And we enjoyed watching the young people participate.

"But look at that older man over there, and that one, and that one," I said as we watched, and none of the older men present were following along. Young Choon who was an excellent missionary then saw quite clearly what was happening and knew if the church was to be kept from becoming only a youth group, he would need to make the worship service so that older men would not feel uncomfortable. Efforts should be made to do all that was possible not to put any kind of barrier up that would make it harder for these men to come to Christ. It was a big step for older Mongolian men to have the courage to even come into a Christian church. The next week the choreography was considerably toned down and Muheen Xair continued to draw older people to its congregation.

Young Mongol believers began attending the new evangelical Bible school called the Union Bible Training Center, UBTC. As a result many smaller churches were sprouting up, usually numbering between twenty and eighty people. It was amazing to see how on fire these young people were for Christ. Often church leaders would attend UBTC during the week, while leading outreaches and church services on Saturdays and Sundays. In the church services, the young Mongol preachers were passionate in their desire to communicate the truths of God to their congregations. Their preaching was dynamic and their singing was dynamic, but without question the strength of the Mongols was evangelism. It seemed to just come naturally to them.

At the same time truly beautiful indigenous music began to be written, produced, and recorded by Mongol believers who were exceptionally gifted in music, and their tapes could be heard playing in homes around the country. With music so dear to the Mongolian heart this especially helped the gospel break through to the people. They were singing their own music, songs written by their own people. It seemed these young believers were aware they were living in an unprecedented time in Mongolian history. The true and living God was moving in a powerful way among the Mongols.

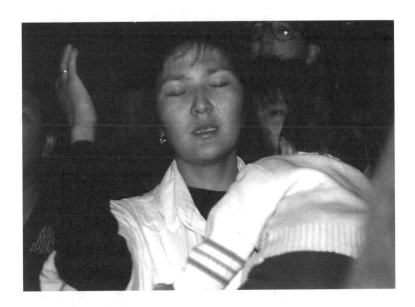

CHAPTER 10

Partnership & A Grain of Wheat

"Unless a grain of wheat falls into the earth and dies it remains alone,
but if it dies, it bears much fruit."
John 12:24

Outside of Mongolia people and organizations were also drawn to
get involved in this far-off land and offer their services for the work
that God was doing among the Mongols. Partnership meetings established by a unique organization called Interdev began in 1991. The first
of these were held in Hong Kong and afterwards in Ulaanbaatar. These
annual gatherings hosted by this neutral organization from the outside
brought the various missionaries and agencies together to work through
differences and find ways of cooperating and working together. At the
meetings everyone could begin to see the bigger picture of what the Lord
was doing and who was working where and how, whether in relief and
development, evangelism, church planting, literature production, radio
broadcasts, translation work or discipleship. Interdev, as well as other
prayer networks around the world, had begun to mobilize prayer against
the powers and principalities of darkness and spiritual forces opposing the
spread of the gospel in Mongolia. It was this concerted prayer that was
paving the way for the amazing breakthroughs we were experiencing.

Even before the diplomatic relationship with the US had been established in 1987, George and Lisa Otis, who in later years became known

for founding The Sentinel Group and making the amazing Transformation videos which have been seen around the world, slipped into Mongolia for a three week reconnaissance mission in 1983. They then wrote the Mongolia Challenge Report which many of us used as a guide in planning our first trips into the country.

In the summer of 1994, the son of the old herdsman who gave Jessica the lamb showed up at our door one day. His name was Inkbat and he had a young wife with him named Saraan Gerel, which in Mongolian means Moonlight. She was called Saraa for short and turned out to be worthy of her name as it is in the Bible. We needed someone to light the fires in the morning the next year for the kindergartens we had started, so we offered the job to Inkbat who promptly gave the job to Saraa as it is generally the woman who lights the fires. We found this out later, and in the meantime, invited them to come live with us in the *hashaa* (fenced in yard) that we had bought.

We had actually bought a couple of *hashaas* next to each other, and taken the fence down in between so that it became one big *hashaa*. The next thing we knew Saraa's family had put up their ger in an empty lot across the dirt alley from us. It turned out that Saraa's father had come from western Mongolia many years before with Inkbat's father. Saraa's father was named Basan (Friday) and he would become my best friend in Mongolia. But the first five times I met Basan he was so drunk he was totally incoherent, and kind of scary, as he would swing and wave his arms dramatically, roaring on and on about whatever it was he was saying.

What we didn't know was that through his stupor, Basan was trying to tell us that long ago when he was a boy, his father had told him that the Americans' God was the true God. His father evidently was one whom the Communists considered a dissident, and they had put him in prison. Basan told us later that he remembered visiting his father while he was in the prison at Uliasti, which is in central Mongolia, and once had been the capitol many years ago. His father died in that prison, so

Basan was not fond of Communism. But before he died, his father had made this statement about the God whom the American people worshipped, and obviously Basan had not forgot. And now, here we were.

And then the startling news came that the old herdsman had died. This was a blow to everyone, as Inkbat's father was known far and wide, having been the country's top yak breeder the year we had met back in 1990. The family, many of whom had been present that day, sent word into town that they would like me to come and conduct the funeral service. It was to be in four days, in order to give friends and relatives from around the country time to travel so they could attend the funeral. We were asked to pick up a family relative who was a professor at one of the colleges in Ulaanbaatar, who wanted to attend the funeral. Besides the professor I asked Boldbaatar to be my translator, and together with Basan, for whom the death of his old friend had brought on a window of sobriety, we headed out to the countryside the night before, as the funeral, by Mongolian custom, would begin at sunrise the next morning.

Other family and friends had already arrived by the time we got there around ten o'clock that night, and the ger was crowded with more than twenty people. It was early December 1994, and the weather was already bitterly cold, fifteen to twenty degrees below zero. We drank some tea and everyone tried to make themselves as comfortable as possible under the conditions of so many people crowded into the ger. Various members of the family and friends would stay up all night chipping away at the frozen earth to make the grave. It was a rough night all the way around.

A few hours later when we awoke, a five ton Russian truck which had brought the casket, was waiting. The body was lying in a small four wall ger, next to the ger where we all slept. Other people had arrived in old Russian jeeps, and by candlelight we now all walked around the body before they placed it in the simple plywood casket, and onto the back of the Russian truck. The dawn was coming now and we could just see the surrounding hills as perhaps a dozen young men climbed aboard the truck. In spite of the cold, they would stand like an honor guard as the old herdsman took his last ride. The other jeeps followed and I brought up the rear in the four-wheel drive Russian van I had bought.

As if in special recognition to the old man because of the great life he had lived, even in this bitter cold, we took a very circuitous route to the cemetery winding cross-country through a valley and over two small mountains. As we drove, I thought back to the day we met, and I had put my arm around the old man and had given him a hug and it had been like grabbing onto a rock. Mongols are the most remarkable people I have met for sheer physical hardiness. After all, these are the people who rode across entire continents when they were on the warpath. And now it was one old warrior's final farewell. It was pretty incredible. There was obviously much symbolism in all the things that were being done, such as the direction and route we took. The temperature was well below zero degrees Fahrenheit, but it seemed that those who stood as the honor guard with the body in the back of the truck wanted to make this sacrifice for their respect of the deceased, and were probably hoping to receive something of the mantle of courage of the one who had died.

After a thirty-minute ride over the hills, we came to the cemetery. The wind was blowing as it had all night long and it was cold. They lowered the casket onto the ground in front of the grave. The grave was not quite yet big enough so they had to chip and dig a bit more. A friend of the family had called for a lama to say prayers over the body. Finally, all was ready and the old lama got out of the truck and walked around the casket with an incense burner swinging from his hand. He said a few prayers, but being a pretty frail old man himself, quickly made his way out of the wind and back to the warmth of the truck.

Boldbaatar nodded that it was my time to speak. I opened the Bible, as it was important that these people saw that I was reading from a Holy Book and not just speaking from my own mind. "I am the bread of life… all that the Father gives Me shall come to Me…and I Myself will raise him up on the last day." I spoke of Christ, of whom most of the people gathered had never heard. I told of His incarnation and mission, and resurrection from the dead for all who would believe. I didn't speak long, as the weather was extremely cold, but then it doesn't take long to bring the good news of the hope in the resurrection.

Someone brought out a piece of paper on which the eulogy was written, and this was read aloud, and a few of the people wept. Mongols rarely show tears but this is one time, if only for a brief moment, that they do. The casket was lowered into the grave and milk was poured over it. Everyone took a handful of dirt and threw it onto the casket. Then everyone took turns with the shovel to fill in the grave. When that was done, we all took rocks that had been brought along in the truck that had brought the casket, and these were placed on the grave until it was completely covered. After a stone marker was set up at the head, we walked three times around the grave. I had us take each other's hands for a final prayer and then we got into the jeeps, trucks, and van, and drove away.

Back at the ger the final part of the funeral was being made ready. This was a meal that everyone would eat together. As we began to eat our soup, they had me sit in the seat of honor across from the door, on the other side of the ger. The ger was quiet. Suddenly I felt the Lord wanted me to speak again as many of the women who were preparing the meal had not been present at the gravesite. I asked permission of the old herdsman's eldest daughter if I might speak and she looked up from her serving with grateful eyes. The ger was full with perhaps forty people pressed inside. And so I began to tell the story of the lost sheep. Since most of these people were shepherds they could relate to Jesus as the Good Shepherd who came to earth looking for his lost sheep. "And now Jesus has brought one of His sheep home," I said. I spoke of the night we met, when Luump had given Jessica the lamb, of how Tenger had become a man, and had died on a cross so that men might be for-given their sins, and the people listened intently just as they had done that first night not far from this very place, when Luump had given his life to Christ. I spoke of the love of God and how He does not want any man to perish but all to put their faith in Christ as the old herdsman had done. There were nods of approval as I finished and the meal went on.

On my left sat the old lama and on my right was a local government official. Bold was seated to the left of the lama, so I asked Bold to ask the lama when he had first heard of Jesus Christ. "Today," came the reply of the old man, "and I greatly liked the things that I heard." At that point the government official spoke up with everyone listening. Bold looked at me and said, "This man is the mayor of the nearby town and he in-vites you to come back and tell his family more about Jesus Christ next summer." Evidently he too wanted to hear more about this man Christ who had risen from the dead.

It had become mid-afternoon and time to go. Usually while visiting the countryside, the van would fill up with people wanting a ride into town, but for some reason that didn't happen today, and there was just Boldbaatar, the professor, Basan, and me. I was driving and Bold was sitting directly behind me on a bench seat that faced the rear. The old professor was sitting across from Bold, and Basan was sitting behind the professor on the rear seat of the van.

"Excuse me," the professor said to Boldbaatar, "but would you mind if I asked you a few questions?"

"Not at all," replied Bold, "go ahead."

"I just want to make sure that I heard correctly what the American said at the gravesite, and then in the ger," he began. "This Jesus whom he was talking about. Did he say that He lived 2000 years ago?"

"That's right," said Bold.

"And did he say that this Jesus is alive right now?"

Bold confirmed that is what I had said, and then being an evangelist in his own right he began to share the gospel for the next hour as we drove back to town. The old professor reminded me of a Nicodemus, an honest scholarly sort with an inquisitive mind.

We got back to town and dropped the professor off at his apartment block, exchanging warm goodbyes with a hope to meet again. Then Bold got out at his apartment building, and Basan and I headed home to our gers.

The next day Basan was still sober and actually doing some work around the hashaa. He had a spring in his step I had not seen before and he seemed to be humming a tune. The next day I spoke to Basan and he had a light in his eyes and a smile on his face. That evening I said to Laura, "Honey, you know I think we ought to talk to Basan about the Lord," and right on cue Basan walked through the door (Mongols do not knock but just come in).

"Basan," I said, "I think it is time for you to know about Jesus Christ."

"Oh, I already do," said Basan.

"What do you mean?" I asked.

"Well you know the other day when we were coming home from the funeral?"

"Yes I remember." I said.

"Don't you remember that Boldbaatar was talking to that man about Jesus," continued Basan. Actually I had forgotten until he brought it up just then.

"Yeah, I remember," I said.

"Well I did it," said Basan.

"You did what?" I asked.

"I told the Lord I was sorry for all the bad things I had ever done and asked him to forgive me, and He did." Basan was very excited, and at the same time, he was at peace. I looked at Laura incredulously, and she at me.

"Praise the Lord," we said, grabbed Basan's hand, and started shaking it in congratulations. There was no doubt about it, Basan was born again just like Jesus said. Wonder of wonders and miracle of miracles! Basan was a new man.

The next thing we knew Basan's whole family believed and we started a small group in our ger. A week later Basan was walking home from the bus stop and met another man whom he invited to come to the meeting that night. Like many men in Mongolia both of these two men struggled with alcoholism. But having received Christ, Basan had now been sober for over a week. The other man's name was Bayarsaihan and his two teenage daughters had recently left home due to his drinking, so he was in a position to listen to some advice. But when he came to the home group that night, he found more than advice. Bayarsaihan experienced love, acceptance, and forgiveness, and he gave his life to Jesus Christ. Bayarsaihan received a new life and went home a changed man.

When he got home, his wife, Altantsag (Golden hour), couldn't even begin to understand what had happened to her husband, and so the next week she came to the home group meeting and there she too received Jesus Christ as her Savior. The next thing they knew, the two daughters who had gone to a town about thirty miles away, heard that their father had met some man named Jesus and was no longer drinking. The girls came home, attended the home group, got saved, went to church, and began going to school again.

Fellowship in the churches was warm and friendly and they steadily grew week by week. But there were also challenges to deal with. One of these was a celebration called *Tsagaan Sar*. *Tsagaan Sar* means White Moon, and is the Mongolian New Year. Truly *Tsagaan Sar* is one of the most beautiful celebrations anywhere in the world. It begins in the morning as whole families are all dressed up in new dells made especially for the occasion, with everyone walking hand in hand to grandmother's house, and then from one family member's house to another... from the grandmother's to the eldest son's, to the next eldest brother, and on down the line. Upon arriving in the home, there is a table set for a king with all of the Mongols' favorite foods set out in a grand display with a big roasted sheep at the end of the table. There was potato salad, sweetened rice with raisins, cabbage salad, meat pies, meat dumplings, milk tea, sweets, etc. It was a feast! However, along with the eating came the drinking, and the Mongols drink vodka... at every house, so that what began as something beautiful in the morning... inevitably ended up by evening a total mess with all the male relatives, uncles, cousins, brothers, along with one's father or grandfather passed out on the floor which had been fully attended by all the chaotic behavior brought on by such drunkenness. Isn't that the devil's way? He comes to kill, to steal, and to destroy.

And so I got Basan, and Bayarsaih and a few other believers who were alcoholic together and held the first AA meeting in Mongolia to talk about their drinking problem. As *Tsagaan Sar* got closer, the men looked as though they were tied to a railroad track with a freight train coming. Could anything be done? The younger men just hung their heads and said, "Nothing."

But Basan spoke up and said there was an ancient custom among the Mongols, that at such a time as when one does not desire to drink, that he can take his ring finger, dip it into the vodka, and touch it to his forehead, signifying that he acknowledged their tradition, and thanks for the offer, but that he didn't want to drink. "Is this right?" I asked. The men reticently nodded in agreement, giving the impression that this was a really old custom and they had never seen it actually done. Instead they were quick to intimate that there would be too much social pressure on them to be able to do such a thing and refuse to drink. They said there is always one person, the most persuasive and forceful family member, appointed to urge all to drink a lot at the feast. Nevertheless I urged them to give what Basan said a try.

Finally *Tsagaan Sar* arrived and Basan invited our family to celebrate *Tsagaan Sar* with his family. As we came into the house of his wife's mother everything was all prepared with the roasted sheep on the living room table with its big white tail of fat hanging over the end. All the important foods were spread out as the old belief was that the more you could put on the table at *Tsagaan Sar,* the more you insured good fortune for your family in the coming year. There were salads and sweets, *boodz* (dumplings) and *hoshur* (fried meat pies).

Milk tea was poured for everyone and then the roasted sheep was cut and the various potato and cabbage salads passed around. Then came the time to drink. The eldest son of the elderly grandmother, began to pour out the vodka in small shot glasses. A glass was passed to Basan and without looking at anyone, he dipped his ring finger in the vodka, flicked it to the left and to the right, as is customary, but then instead of downing the vodka, he touched his ring finger to his forehead, and picked up the knife to cut some meat, still not looking at anyone. Nevertheless his abstinence did not go unnoticed.

From there the family went to the elder brother's house and once again the living room table was set out in the same fashion as it had been at the grandmother's. They drank the tea, ate the sheep, the salads, the sweets, the *boodz,* the *hoshur,* and then once again the vodka was poured.

The glasses were filled and again one was pushed towards Basan. This time his hand was shaking and moved slowly to receive the vodka, but then as everyone watched, Basan dipped his finger in the vodka, flicked it into the air in the customary way, and touched his hand to his head as reverently as possible. Now there was no mistaking the fact that Basan was not drinking! One of the brothers tried to insist, but Basan was older than him, and simply raised his hand in such a way as to peacefully communicate that he would not drink. What made all of this so totally remarkable was that Basan had been leading this little party for the last thirty-five years! Yet now the star performer was not taking the stage.

A strong message was being communicated to an entire family in a powerful way because it was taking place in their own cultural patterns and customs. Things would never be the same. It is so important to keep new believers in the warp and woof of the social fabric of the culture. To take them out contradicts the great commandment, breaks relationships, and therefore the natural spontaneous spread of the gospel.

In the years to come, more and more men in the church learned how to handle *Tsagaan Sar*. In addition to using the ancient custom Basan invoked, one young pastor remembered another tradition from the days of Genghis Khan, where the men under the age of forty were not allowed to drink at all. Men between forty and fifty years old were allowed just a little, and those older than fifty were supposed to know how to control themselves. At *Tsagaan Sar* the young believers would recall this ancient tradition of the Mongol people, and as a consequence found yet another way to protect themselves and others, from the destructiveness of alcohol. In time, the church would begin to look forward to *Tsagaan Sar* as a time when a Christian witness could be communicated to yet unsaved family members. God is good.

Inner healing was a big need in Mongolia. Revenge, rather than forgiveness, had been the way of the Mongols. Some parts of a culture can be redeemed, but obviously some parts must be transformed. Much bitterness seemed to be inside of many of the people, and I would often give an invitation for them to come forward at the end of a service to be set free from the bondage the devil wanted to continue to hold them in. These were precious times as people submitted themselves to God.

The Mongol people were spiritually hungry. What an amazing transformation happened when they would surrender all that grief and pent-up hatred toward a relative, an abusive father, or whoever it was who had wronged them, and forgive. Sometimes they would say they couldn't forgive so it was important to make it clear that the choice was theirs. Often they would then break down and begin to weep tears that needed to have flown years before. But those tears brought freedom, and the wonderful blessing of restored relationships, and that is what life is all about. It happened over and over again as people yielded to the Holy Spirit who reconciled these men and women to the Lord Jesus Christ, who had so graciously become their Healer, their Savior, and their God. Jesus was real, the true God who had created the world, and who loved them… and they had come to know Him and love Him.

Evangelistic outreaches began to go further and further afield. I sent Basan and Bayarsaihan on the trains up and down the railroad line that ran from China to Russia. They passed out a little tract called *Life's Golden Secret*, along with the Gospels of John and Mark. Basan and Bayarsaihan would then begin witnessing on the trains while passing out the books. One week they would go south, and the next week they would go north. It was hard work as the trains were always very crowded, but the two of them put their hearts into it. The ministry they conducted bore much fruit over the years, as they sowed the word of God up and down the railroad line.

One time I went with them and we stopped in the little town of Choir, about halfway between Ulaanbaatar and the Chinese border. That night we held a meeting, and a little woman whose heart the Lord had prepared beforehand, gave her life to Christ. As we began to drink tea with the family, the team was witnessing to the woman's grown son, a man in his late thirties who was also there. The old woman was sitting in the corner fingering her beads, as religious Mongols often do. Buddhists use the beads to count their prayers just like Catholics. The Holy Spirit showed me that her fingering her beads simply meant that she was interested in God, and that I should talk to the woman. She listened intently for half an hour and finally, upon understanding that the good news of Christ was a free gift, she shouted, "*Awen, awen, tigelgui yakov* (I'll take it, I'll take it, it can be no other way)." And with that cry from the depths of her heart the old woman was changed in a moment of time. It was like someone had pulled the plug on a sink full of dirty water, and all that old water went out the drain, and in its place was clear, fresh, living water. Her face was radiant, almost like she was an angel. It was amazing! A few minutes later the old lady said, "I have been looking for God all of my life and now I have found him." Many such stories could be told as the gospel spread among the Mongols.

Basan and my father

CHAPTER 11

Burkhan & The Master of the Universe

"In the beginning was the logos,
and the logos was with Theos, and the logos was Theos."
John 1:1

The Mongolian translation of the New Testament, had come out in August of 1990, just as the first resident missionaries arrived in Mongolia. With the translation backed by a Bible Society, everyone naturally expected that it was an accurate translation of God's word, and proceeded to use it with that in mind. The problem was that in 1990 when the translation was published, there was only one other missionary at that time who knew Mongolian well enough to be able to check the translator's work, and the Bible Society evidently did not know this man. However by 1993, a number of other missionaries had learned to read Mongolian and were beginning to find significant mistakes in the New Testament that had been published. Inaccuracies in the translation began to dominate conversation in the mission community. Often a missionary would be trying to lead a Bible study and their translator would look up from searching his Mongolian New Testament and say, "What you are saying is not written in our book."

Reading this translation was a little like reading a commentary. The translator had been in and out of Mongolia in the 1970s studying the language on academic exchanges from England. Most of the translation had then been done in England in the 1980s and the translator was not ancticipating that things would open up in Mongolia as they did, and so he included as much commentary in his translation as he could. But it would have been better had the translator put his commentary as footnotes at the bottom of the page rather than intertwining them in the text itself. To mix the two is not acceptable, for it is the Word of God that has the power to change men, and not man's explanation of it. The result was the young Mongol believers were not remembering or memorizing Scripture. Why not? People do not memorize commentaries. Furthermore the believers were having trouble with the notion of daily Bible reading, which the missionaries urged upon them. They contended that they had already read it all and couldn't see any value in endless rereadings. Again people do not continually read and memorize commentaries.

The missionaries who had come to Mongolia to win the lost and make disciples now faced a dilemma. What were they to do? Another year went by and the church continued to be made up mostly of young teenagers who were wonderfully exuberant and zealous, but greatly lacking in spiritual growth. The translation was also weak on an accurate translation of sexual immorality. Some of the young men who were leaders in the early church, confessed years later, to the sexual sin in which they were regularly engaging, while earlier in the day they were standing before a congregation. As a result, one young church leader after another fell into sexual immorality, and pregnancy followed pregnancy. The overall effect of the 1990 translation, seemed to convey the message from the Biblical story about the woman caught in adultery of Jesus saying, "Neither do I condemn you," but was weak in expressing, "Go and sin no more."

Besides the inaccuracy of the translation, the translator failed to use the traditional Mongolian word for God, *Burkhan*. Instead the translator chose a term that literally means, "Master of the Universe," which he found in a dictionary published in 1968. This was not a common word among Mongols and most of them had never heard of it. For many older Mongols, this term "Master of the Universe" sounded made up, like a kind of science fiction hero.

Furthermore this obscure word carried a somewhat different connotation than that of "God," and of course that didn't sit well with missionaries. And when Mongolian Christians began to read the Bible in other languages such as Russian, German, English, Korean, or any other language, and compared their book to others, they quickly saw that the name for God in their Bible was not the same as in other translations. For instance, they would read in German that "In the beginning *Gott* created the heavens and the earth," or in Russian they could read that "*Boag* created the heavens and the earth," and they all knew that the equivalent of these terms in Mongolian was *Burkhan*.

The term *Burkhan* in Mongolian, would be similar in meaning to the word *Theos* in Greek, which all of the writers used for God in the New Testament. Though the New Testament writers were all Jews with the possible exception of Luke, they did not use the Hebrew words for God, such as *Yahweh, El Shaddai,* or *El Elyon.* Instead under the guidance of the Holy Spirit, they used the Greek word *Theos.* Most theologians and missiologists believe that in doing this God was making a statement, that this gospel that was to go into all the world should do so via the language and terminology of the local people and even the very word for God was to be translated using their languages as it had been in Greek.

In the summers of 1992 and 1993, as the JESUS film, which used the unfamiliar terminology of the Bible Society translation, began to be shown around the countryside, many Mongols simply did not understand what was being talked about, as they had never heard of the 'Master of the Universe.' After the film was shown, a Mongol Christian would invariably have to stand up and explain the movie using the traditional Mongolian term for God of *Burkhan*. "Oh, you are talking about God," the Mongols would then say. "Why didn't you say so in the first place?"

In the first Bible school that had been started, one of the Mongol church leaders was interpreting for a visiting teacher from the U.S. When the students did not understand the meaning of the American instructor's teaching because the Mongol interpreter tried to use the terminology of the Mongol New Testament, the young Mongol translating then switched to traditional Mongolian terminology to get the point across. That worked perfectly well and everyone in the class understood what was being said.

Back in 1990, before the translation came out, when the old herdsman in the ger gave my daughter Jessica the lamb, the translator had naturally used *Burkhan*, except for the times I specifically referred back to the ancient term for God of *Tenger*, and the Mongols had no misunderstanding about what was being said.

It seemed since the average man on the street knew God as *Burkhan*, and the word used on television, radio, and in the newspapers was *Burkhan*, it would make sense to use this term. The whole culture knew God as *Burkhan*. All two million Mongols in Outer Mongolia, plus three million Mongols down in Inner Mongolia of China, and the one million Mongols up in Russia, all called God by the name, *Burkhan*.

For many Mongols, when "Master of the Universe" was used, the issue was no longer a matter of who was the true God, for Jesus was no longer being presented to them as *Burkhan* with a capital B. Instead, as the Master of the Universe, Jesus became just another *burkhan* (small b) to add to their many other *burkhans*, this one called, "Master of the Universe."

Another major factor that became evident was that the term, "Master of the Universe," was primarily attracting teenagers who were ready to accept and believe most anything that came out of the West. However the message was not reaching the adult Mongol. In 1994 when the number of Christians had reached a couple of thousand, the average age of the church member was only around seventeen, with many thirteen to sixteen year olds making up much of the congregations. So the church was essentially a very large youth group, as the gospel, with its strange "Master of the Universe" terminology, sounding quite foreign to most mature Mongols. The mainstream of Mongol society was simply not responding. There were a few older people who came to the Lord and were attending the churches, but by and large, the church in Mongolia at this time was comprised of very young people.

The gospel however is for all people, and must be understood by young and old alike, educated and uneducated, herder and scholar. Since the entire Mongolian nation used the word *Burkhan*, as evangelists, most missionaries were more concerned in what word would communicate and connect with the common people, rather than debating over an obscure word which no one used or had ever heard of that had been found in a dictionary.

Only these very young new Christians in Outer Mongolia, called God by the name, "Master of the Universe," and this was perfectly understandable. Why shouldn't they? That was the word written in the book they had been given. Why wouldn't it be correct? But the missionaries with greater perspective and understanding, while rejoicing with these young people who had responded to the Lord, along with the few older ones, were also thinking about the millions of Mongols who were not responding to the message. The question was, if the Mongol Christians had a chance to choose which word they wanted, what word would they use?

Then in November of 1993, there was yet another discussion on the translation issue. Surely this would be just one more meeting on the subject. There were only a few people present, a German, a Japanese, a Korean, and a couple of Americans. And so they drank tea and started talking covering well-known territory once again. Then as the conversation continued, someone suggested that what was needed was a brand new translation, and that a committee should be formed to produce it, and suddenly the conversation turned serious.

"Do you mean start an entire translation project?" one person asked rather incredulously, as this was something he had never thought of doing. Most of them were evangelists or pastors and simply wanted to win people to Christ and make disciples. But everyone had to admit it was pretty hard to make disciples, or even to try to lead a Bible study using the present translation. The room became silent.

Probably none of those who were there that day came with the idea that they were going to start a translation committee. Perhaps the one who had called the meeting did, but this wasn't something most of them expected. However with the idea of forming a committee on the table before the directors of five mission agencies, a sense of purpose and destiny seemed to come into our midst, and we began to talk about what would be needed to start a new translation project.

Probably none of us knew what we were getting into that day. But everyone knew something needed to be done and it looked like we were the ones the Lord was calling to do it. In a few days another meeting was held and a couple of Mongols who were particularly gifted in translating joined the group. Other meetings followed and as the calendar turned to 1994, the Mongolian Bible Translation Committee had come into being.

A year later the MBTC produced its first books of John and Mark in May of 1995. Boldbaatar, who had heard the gospel from Native Americans back in 1990 and helped baptize the thirty-four believers in 1991, became the translator of the New Testament. In the course of translating the Scriptures the MBTC hosted five open meetings with the Christian community, discussing the various issues surrounding the translation and the terminology. After hearing our explanations, churches began to agree with the more literal translation we were producing and the use of traditional Mongolian terminology, the various mission organizations began using our books in their outreaches.

Basan's wife Sambo

CHAPTER 12

A Love Story in Erdenet

"Behold, I will do a new thing,
now it will spring forth, will you not be aware of it?"
Isaiah 43:19

The train pulled out of the station in Ulaanbaatar at 7:20 p.m. and would travel through the night to the city of Erdenet. Most people on the train brought their dinner and enjoyed the view of the countryside during the summer as the engine pulled them forward past flocks and streams, herds and hills, past people living where there were no roads whose children stood waving at the train as it chugged along into the approaching night. It was a beautiful journey I made many times, as did others whom the Lord would call to Erdenet, as He began to move dramatically in this small mining town of 65,000 people.

The church was started in January 1993, with the baptism of fourteen teenage girls, which was not exactly the most auspicious beginning for a church, but then the Lord's ways are higher than ours. Though He obviously knew that girls would bring boys, there were other factors that entered in as the Holy Spirit moved in an extraordinary way through signs and wonders with some dramatic healings taking place, and after only one year the baptized believers totaled one hundred and twenty.

The church was pioneered by the Swedish missionary whom I had first seen with his eyes up and arms outstretched to God, praying before a room jam-packed with people, and yet you could have heard a pin drop. Magnus Alphonce and his wife Maria were joined a year later by Brian and Louise Hogan and their three daughters from the U.S., and then a Russian couple a year after that, followed by a single fellow from the U.S. and finally another Swede.

Here in Erdenet it seemed the Lord had decided He would create a love story of His own design. Amazingly, the church in Erdenet grew and grew until it became the largest church in Mongolia. As a consequence there were plenty of marriages among the many young Mongols who would meet each other in the church. Love is a relationship and so is the Church.

It is not often that a church plant in a completely untouched field is worthy of being written up as an actual case study for missionaries all over the world, but that is exactly what happened in Erdenet. It was as if all the blood, sweat, and tears of all the years of experience from the apostle Paul to Hudson Taylor to the present day would find expression in this amazing move of God. From the very beginning, the most up-to-date missiology was not only talked about but put into practice, and lo and behold, it worked. Bonding, contextualization, indigenization, training national leaders, instilling a vision for outreach and multiplication throughout the country and for missions abroad beyond the borders of Mongolia, and planning an exit strategy from the very beginning, for the missionaries to leave after the church had its own Mongolian leadership capable of upholding the standard and purposes of God. These were all part of the dynamics that went into the church in Erdenet. And of course lots and lots of love.

The missionaries whom the Lord brought together to form the team were gifted and committed, and their gifts and commitment complimented one another's. They were courageous and they were caring, they wept with those who wept, and they rejoiced with those who rejoiced, as one person after another in Erdenet received forgiveness of sins and was set free from the shackles of Satan. The Lord was building a church in Erdenet that would display His glory, and like no other church in the country at that time, this church began to penetrate into the mainstream of Mongolian society.

One of the great strengths of the church was that it was founded on the model of a cell church and met in homes and not just in a building. In the cell groups, the priesthood of the believers found full expression as the new believers were trained in how to minister to one another. This also allowed the church to maintain continuity and growth even when the government would force its larger meetings out of one building to another, or even completely prevent them for a time, as was common in all of the Mongolian churches. So the church would continue to grow in the cells, and therefore continued to grow in the large group meetings as well.

But it was probably the worship and the creativity of the church in Erdenet that began to distinguish it as something unique. Dramatizations of the gospel were acted out during Sunday morning celebration meetings with such a fervency by the young believers that it transformed doctrine into reality. This helped people to not only understand the forgiveness of Christ in everyday life, but to experience the freedom that forgiveness

Brian and Louise Hogan with team members in Erdenet.

brings as they would come forward for ministry during the services and be touched by the wonderful reality which life in Christ has to offer.

The worship team in Erdenet seemed to have absorbed the best of everything around the world and brought it under the Lordship of Christ and the authority of the Holy Spirit. The result was power, passion, exuberance, and a joy unspeakable that was filled with glory! How amazing to walk into wherever the church happened to be meeting, and see hundreds of people, young and old, dancing with the music, much of which was written by the believers themselves, rather than translations of western choruses.

And then came the test. The church's worship leader fell into sin. It was a single incident, just one mistake as old friends had persuaded her to attend a party. It was not an ongoing affair, just a single slip, but it happened, and the young worship leader was devastated. But by the grace of God, and the discipling she had so far received, the worship leader came to the missionaries and confessed her sin in great brokenness, sobbing and weeping as did everyone else. What to do now? Some churches in Ulaanbaatar tended to overlook sexual lapses as almost something to be expected, and therefore had often tried to hide the sin, in hopes that nobody else would find out and they could keep their leader in place and go on. But this only weakens a church, never strengthens it.

It was obvious that this beautiful young woman in her early twenties was broken, repentant, and possibly no one else would have known what had happened, as she had come first to the mission team and poured her heart out. But God knew, and the girl knew, and for her sake, as well as the church's, according to the word of God, something had to be done. If there was no discipline, where was the real love that was being taught? And so, as painful and difficult as it was, the missionaries called the church leadership together, and shared what had happened. And though the result was that the worship leader was removed from her position, at the same time, she remained in close fellowship with both the missionaries and the Mongol church leadership. They were still one. The disciplinary probation from public ministry put into effect by the church's leadership would be for a six-month period! Not for just a week or two, as had been done in other churches who were eager to keep their leaders in their position, but for six whole months!

But it was the way the discipline was administered that is the important lesson here. The missionaries wisely did not tell the Mongol leadership what to do, but instead they shared the problem and pointed them to the Scriptures. Though the missionary may know what needs to happen, it is not often that he has the presence of mind not to give the answer, but to ask the question, "What does God's word say about this?" The approach demands the missionary to trust the Holy Spirit's ability to communicate to His people. Two things then happen at once. Firstly, the immediate problem at hand is solved based on Scripture. Secondly, the situation serves as a model in training the church leaders to turn to the Scriptures for their answers, and not to the missionary, thus insuring the future of the church. Perhaps this as much as anything drew the hand of God upon this church in a marvelous way, and began to form it into what could truly be called an indigenous church.

The definition of an indigenous church has been given as one that is self-governing, self-supporting, and self-propagating, sometimes referred to as "The Three Selfs," and certainly all of those things are needed. But this definition is incomplete because the focus is on the external outworking of administration, financing, and reproduction. Beyond these rudimentary prerequisites, a truly indigenous church is one that knows how to search the Scriptures, how to interpret the Scriptures, and how to apply the Scriptures. These, together with the other things, are what it takes to plant an indigenous church. God always blesses obedience to His word! The missionaries in Erdenet had taught the church how to search, interpret, and apply the Scriptures. It was the Mongolian church leaders who exercised the disciplinary action, after careful study and interpretation of the Scriptures.

Six months later this young woman was reinstated and became one of the most dynamic worship leaders in the country, as her feet hardly touched the stage when she led the congregation in praise. This young woman now knew the grace of God from both sides of the fence like few others. She had sinned, she had been forgiven and disciplined, and now had a love for Christ that could not be extinguished. She was on fire and that fire was beautiful and contagious. Her love for Jesus Christ radiated forth every Sunday morning for all to see, and the powers and principalities of darkness had no hold on her. She was free and now there was no turning back.

Another one of the key factors that brought forth the breakthrough in Erdenet and allowed the movement to reach mainstream Mongolian society was that the church there used the traditional Mongolian word of *Burkhan* for God. This enabled everyone, old and young, to know just Whom was being talked about and worshipped. This was the God who had created the world. This was reality, not religion.

And finally the missionaries in Erdenet planned the end from the beginning. In April of 1996, a formal ceremony took place as the missionaries literally passed a baton to the Mongolian church leaders signifying that they were now the leaders of the church. And with that the missionaries in Erdenet began to take their leave of a place and people to whom they had given their lives. This example proved to be a key in the future outreaches and church plants that came forth from the mother church known as the Jesus Assembly in Erdenet.

The goal of missions is to establish within each people group, indigenous church movements worshipping God in spirit and in truth which are capable of multiplying congregations so that the entire people group is evangelized and brought into fellowship. If an indigenous church is the goal, then contextualization is the means to that end. Therefore the task of the missionary is to just bring the simple gospel and as little of their own cultural and ecclesiological background as possible. What are needed are indigenous churches, not denominational churches of the missionary's background, but rather national churches where the Holy Spirit is free to express Himself within the heart-language and culture of each people group. Too often in many countries where the gospel has long been standing, the churches reflect more of a denominational expression. Denominations are fine, but they do not need to be exported. The gospel, not the way one does church back home, is what needs to be communicated.

There was something quite unique in the atmosphere of Mongolia in the 1990s. Walking down the streets in Ulaanbaatar, the air was crisp and charged with the energy that something special was happening in Mongolia. Many people realized this and took their shoes off, in a spiritual sense, when they came into the country. Many recognized that it was God who was at work in Mongolia, and they set aside their own personal agendas to see how they were to fit into His plan for the nation. The Holy Spirit was sweet, and greatly honored those who came to do the will of God, whatever His will might be. Mongolia might not be everybody's cup of tea, but for those who had answered the call of God, and were there at His command, nowhere else could compare. For a missionary, Mongolia was a great place to be in that very last decade of the twentieth century.

CHAPTER 13

Koreans, Germans, & Kindergartens

"Therefore accept one another,
as Christ also has accepted you."
Romans 15:7

Unity can be an elusive goal. Back home we often think of apathy as the big problem of the church. But on the mission field apathy is not the problem, as missionaries and new believers are usually highly motivated people. But getting all of those highly motivated people to work together can sometimes be like herding cats.

Most of our sermons on unity come from John 17:21-23. But this marvelous passage simply tells us that we need unity, that we are perfected in unity, and that the world will know that God sent Christ when we are united. But it doesn't tell us how to achieve unity.

However, a passage from the book of Romans solves the mystery and tells us how to achieve unity. Like on most mission fields, we struggled to find unity in Mongolia, whether over methodology, or terminology, or some other issue. As one of the leaders I continued to search the Scriptures for the secret until one day the Lord opened my eyes to see Romans 15:7 in a new light. As I sat in my room looking at this verse, the Holy Spirit led me to see that here was the key. "Therefore accept one another, just as Christ also has accepted you."

Could it be that easy? The difficulty seemed to lie in the "accepting." How do you accept someone with whom you disagree? The answer comes from the will. You choose to. There is no reason why we should allow differences to disrupt unity in the body of Christ. One group may believe that baptism should be by immersion, another group might think it is also permissible to pour water over the believer's head. Is this difference any reason why we cannot accept each other as Christ has accepted us? No. If a person is born again of the spirit of Jesus Christ, he or she is my brother or sister, whether they were baptized this way or that, whether they believe we must all speak in tongues or don't believe that, whether we want to use this term and another wants to use that term. We can still be one in Christ by choosing to accept one another as Christ has accepted us. It is an act of the will. We choose to accept each other, and so we are one in spirit though perhaps we differ regarding externals. As the saying goes, "In essentials unity, in non-essentials liberty, in all things charity."

One of the most integral dynamics to the opening of Mongolia and the establishing of the church was the influence of the Korean mission community. Not only were they the most numerous (about one-third) of all the foreign missionaries who had come to Mongolia, they were also the most highly trained in theology. Lay ministry is not as big in Korea as it is in the United States and other countries, and many of the Koreans who came to Mongolia had full Master of Divinity degrees from seminaries, and many were ordained ministers.

The Koreans enjoyed the blessing of having a similar language to the Mongolians. It turned out that the Korean and Mongolian languages are grammatically structured the same. This is was a tremendous advantage as they simply had to learn new vocabulary, and substitute it into the sentence structure they already knew, whereas the westerner had to learn a complete new way of thinking. The Koreans quickly learned the

Mongolian language and were often preaching within six months to a year of arrival in Mongolia. Being highly disciplined and good students, they picked up new words everyday and improved in their speaking quite rapidly.

As a result, many of the churches were led by Korean missionaries. However, a problem emerged, for though the two languages were structured the same, the cultures were just the opposite. While the Koreans are extremely vertical, having top-down authority structures and thought patterns, the Mongols are the epitome of an egalitarian society where everyone is equal. The gifted Koreans had much knowledge, discipline, and graciousness to offer, but they needed to learn to present these gifts in a Mongolian way, which was not always easy for them to do.

The problem was that though the Koreans were well trained in theology, they were not well trained in missions and brought with them the form and structure of church which they had experienced in Korea. As the number of believers in Korea now totals more than thirty-nine percent of their total population, they are obviously doing many things right. However, it was the same principle of indigenous leadership which had produced the tremendous growth of the church in the Korea that needed to be taught to the Mongols, and not the subsequent hierarchical structure, rigid control, and formal worship of the Korean church.

And so a tension developed between the Mongol leadership and the Korean leaders. There was the obvious need for the church to be Mongolian. However, the need for the contextualization of the gospel to meet the Mongol culture was very difficult for many of the Koreans to receive. The new wine of Mongolian believers needed new wine skins to contain the emerging Mongol church. If old wineskins (structures) were used to try to contain the new wine of the Mongol church, they would break. The Korean missionary leaders struggled with the tension as did the young Mongolian leaders. No doubt the Koreans felt that to be placed in a position of leadership the Mongols should go through seminary training such as they had received back in Korea. The Mongol leadership was young and inexperienced, this was true, but holding them back for lack of seminary training was counter-productive and not the way to proceed in Mongolia. The job of the missionary is to equip the church to carry the King, to teach them and disciple them until they are mature enough to stand firm in the Lord, proclaim the gospel, follow correct doctrine, and live righteously.

Consequently by 1996, young Mongolian church leaders were struggling with the Korean pastor they were serving under. Getting up at 6 a.m. to come to prayer meeting and working seven days a week were not the way Mongols were built. Nor was unquestioning submission to authority such as the Koreans were used to. But the Mongol church leaders had things to learn from their Korean pastors, and most chose to stay under their spiritual authority though it was difficult. Their hearts were right.

In August of 1997, a German organization initiated a high profile conference, renting the Sports Palace where the Mongolian wrestling championships were held, and brought in speakers from abroad. In preparation for the conference they took the time to meet with the leaders of other mission organizations, and the Mongolian leaders of the emerging church, inviting everyone to work together. As a result, close to three thousand Christians gathered at the conference. Unity! This was the largest gathering of the body of Christ the church had yet seen. The Lord was moving through the different expressions of His body and building His church.

The highlight of the conference came when one of the visiting speakers prophesied that "though the Mongols were once not His people, that they were now becoming the people of God." This was followed by the prophecy that the Mongols would once again go forth over the lands they had conquered seven hundred years ago, but this time carrying the message of salvation. This prophetic word was anointed and a great cry of affirmation went up from the people.

And though this had certainly been said before in private conversations by many who were living in Mongolia, this conference was the first time a public proclamation was made that the Mongols would once again go forth from their country, over the land that Genghis Khan had conquered, but this time bearing the gospel of Jesus Christ to reconcile men to God. This was a sobering moment as the people who were gathered there that day realized that God had a plan and a destiny for them to fulfill.

In the 1990s, Ulaanbaatar was a city of somewhere around 800,000, which was roughly one-third of the total population of Mongolia. In the center of the city were the government buildings, hotels, the opera house, theaters, gift shops, and museums, surrounded by apartment buildings, grocery stores, clothing shops, etc. And then there were the ger communities with many poor people surrounding the city.

From the seventh floor window of our flat, we could see the ger districts stretching out to the north. They were a maze of dirt alleys and wooden fences and power poles with wires everywhere bringing people the electricity that was being generated by the huge coal burning power plant on the west side of town. They had no running water or indoor plumbing and so everyone had their own outhouse. To say these people were poor would be a great understatement. They were destitute.

It was to the poor people in these ger communities that Laura and I felt drawn. So one day we took a translator into one of the ger districts and asked the people if we supplied kindergarten education for their children using a ger for a classroom, would they be interested? One of the first things to be cut when the Communist era ended and budgets were slashed, was kindergarten education for the poor. So of course the people were interested in what we said, and began to tell us that long ago there had been kindergartens in gers. So I asked them if we were to do this, where would they want to put the school? That caught them off guard. I was asking them, rather than telling them what to do, and in a moment a new excitement came into their eyes as they saw that we were not there to try to control them, but simply wanted to help them. And so I explained that the kindergarten we had in mind would be something of a community project. I would supply the ger but they would need to supply stools for the children to sit on, (which I knew were common in the ger community). It was to be a kind of joint venture, and everyone liked the idea.

The kindergartens we had started were dynamic as our teachers Delgurmaa, Toogsmaa, and Oyun were all new believers and really gave themselves to their work, and the parents of the children were appreciative. Our goal was to love the kids more than educate them. One little boy came to us who looked to be a cross of Mongol and Russian. He had obviously gone through his share of teasing in life and was therefore reserved and withdrawn. But love never fails and within a couple of weeks he was running and playing with the other kids like he had never done before.

Once they got to know us and saw the results that were taking place, the parents actually asked if we would teach ethics and morals to their children. However I was careful not to use our kindergartens as a kind of Sunday school to teach religion, which would have been against the law.

Noona

Finally the government heard about our kindergartens and the Minister of Education asked to see me. By now I had befriended an elderly woman named Noona, who was the most well known kindergarten teacher in all of Mongolia. Noona had given us great advice in setting up our kindergartens, and so I asked her to come along. When the Minister of Education saw that Noona was sitting on our side of the table, our credibility soared without a word being spoken.

"Hello," I said in Mongolian, "How are you?" And the minister answered, "Fine, how are you?" So I proceeded on with the same protocol of greeting I had first learned back in 1988. "How is your health? How is your family? How are your wife and children? What's new?" I had since learned that if I asked "How are your cattle" to a city person they would usually start laughing, so I would only use this when in a rural context.

The minister was impressed, and then together with Noona and my interpreter we talked about kindergarten education. The minister expressed his gratitude for our help and I told him we were glad to do it. I told him we were holding our kindergartens in gers and were hoping to develop a model which could be used all over the country. And indeed, other organizations, quickly picked up on the idea, and started kindergartens as well.

At the close of our meeting, the Minister of Education looked at me and asked the tell tale question, "Mr. Leatherwood, do you teach religion in your kindergartens?"

"No sir we don't," I said, looking him in the eye, "but I am a Christian and I do believe that a man has risen from the dead." After letting that thought settle in his mind for a moment I continued on, "The parents of our kindergartens have asked us to teach morals and ethics such as people should not steal, and should not lie, should not be mean and things like this, but that we should be kind to one another, and so we do teach these kind of things, and we also would like to put on a Christmas program."

The interview with the Minister of Education went well and once again I felt I had made a friend. I could tell that both Noona and Dageema, the very sharp young woman who was translating for me, had been extremely pleased with my complete candidness with the Minister about what we were doing in the kindergartens. The Mongols had dealt in a system of lies for seventy years and were watching closely to see if we missionaries really practiced what we were preaching. It was through opportunities like this that we could show them that we must walk our talk and be truthful. Principles and doctrines are dead if they are not consistently applied in life.

Delgurma

The Christmas program was certainly the real thing. We had an outdoor manger scene with live animals (not too hard to arrange), and the kindergarten children acted out a little drama with Mary and Joseph, the shepherds, the wise men, and the angels. To conclude the program I told the Christmas story to try to fill in the blanks and explained the birth of Christ two thousand years ago.

With the temperature at zero degrees Fahrenheit the reenactment was a little colder than what had taken place in Bethlehem, but it seemed to work out pretty well.

Afterwards, we went into the ger for a traditional Mongolian meal which the parents had brought of traditional meat dumplings called *boedz*, (long o on the vowel), cabbage salad (coleslaw), cucumbers, tomatoes, milk tea (lots of this), cake, candy, and cookies just as might have been at any Mongolian school in the country. And so the Lord gave us favor with the people as we were gaining their trust more and more, and they truly appreciated the school.

The other surprise was when I said my family owned a ger and would like to come and live with them. I asked if anyone had a *hashaa* we could live in and there was a moment of silence. Then a man who was standing there said we were welcome to put up our ger in his *hashaa*.

Eyebrows went up in the mission community when it was learned that we had moved into the ger community. However it has been my experience that to the degree that you immerse yourself into a culture, the greater you come to appreciate the beauty and the richness that God has put in that culture. And likewise the people come to appreciate you.

In mission terminology it is called bonding, and is a key to becoming accepted as an insider in the culture. And it is when one becomes an insider that others listen more closely to what is being said. The more one can do things the way the local people do them, both you and your message will be accepted. The old saying, "when in Rome, do as the Romans do" is true, and to the degree that we eat their food, observe their customs, and honor their traditions, as long as sin is not involved, friendships can be built, and love is communicated without a word being said.

We decided we would set up two gers that were connected together. This was an idea that was a little unconventional, so again I sought the approval of the Mongols nearby. They all said no problem and one of the men standing there who was a carpenter and also something of an artist said he could make the door frame needed to connect the two gers. It was really quite nice when he got it done and we put our two gers together connected by the doorway. To do so we simply separated the fourth and fifth walls of the first ger, and set the frame the carpenter had made for us, into the opening. Then we turned the second ger ninety degrees so that the door of this second ger fit into the specially made frame of the first, thereby connecting the two.

And so we moved into a ger which was really a great experience for our whole family. Daniel was our oldest son who had just turned ten, and it was his job each day to get water for us. This was not an easy task after it had rained or snowed as he had to push the dolly a quarter of a mile with a twenty-liter canister on it and the mud would make it hard slogging. David and Jonathan our twins, were turning eight, and their job was to get the coal from the shed and bring it into the ger, and Jessica at four years old, enjoyed being too young to work.

That first winter in the ger, the snow drifted up over the two meter high fence (though the snow was only a couple of inches in the open field) and so the boys made tunnels and caves in the drift. The main sport in winter for all the children in the area was sliding down the mountain at the end of our dirt street on a sled which could range from a real sled with runners, to something as simple as a piece of cardboard or sheet of hard plastic.

A church in Colorado sent an amazing woman named Helen Richardson to tutor our kids and help in the kindergartens. Our favorite pastime as a family was reading together in the evenings. Our favorite books were J.R.R. Tolkein's *The Hobbit*, and *The Lord of the Rings*. Often

Helen Richardson

we had barely finished dinner when the kids would want to start the story, so I would read as Laura did the dishes. One of the advantages to living in a ger is that the kitchen, the living room, the dining room and the den are all in the same room. So the first winter we read *The Hobbit* and the Tril-

ogy and the next winter we read C.S. Lewis' *Chronicles of Narnia*, and kept up this practice for the next seven years. Looking back on it now, I cannot think of a better thing for parents to do than turn off the TV set and read to their children.

A few days after we moved into the ger, I came home and there seemed to be a lot of people standing outside our ger. At first I was alarmed that something might be wrong, but then I saw the TV cameras. News had gotten out about the Americans who were living in a ger! So here was the national broadcasting station, Mongol TV, with one of their film crews, and they wanted to know if they could have an interview. So after greetings, I invited them in and Laura served tea, as I sat down and started to answer their questions.

"How did we like living in Mongolia?

"Wasn't it hard for an American to live in a ger?

"Did we think the situation in Mongolia was difficult?

"Where did our children go to school?

"What were our impressions of Mongolia?"

The Mongols had been locked away from the rest of the world for almost seventy years, and they were curious about everything. At this point their economy was at rock bottom so that not too many Mongols had yet traveled abroad to the West, so they were interested to know what other people thought of them.

We said yes we were very happy to be in Mongolia and enjoyed living in a ger. Our kids could play outside without having to go down seven flights of stairs onto a crowded street and they could go sledding with the other children in the community. And we considered it a privilege to serve the Mongol people during this time of transition in which they now found themselves. Finally they asked, "How long do you plan to stay in Mongolia?" and that was the question I was hoping for because it gave me an opportunity to bring the Lord into the conversation in a natural way saying that our time in Mongolia was up to Him and we would stay as long as He wanted us to stay. I listened carefully to the word for God their translator used, who was interpreting for the interviewer, and of course it was *Burkhan*.

It was getting cool and as Laura hadn't had time to start the fire yet, I went outside for a moment to chop some wood. This was a big hit as they saw us doing things just like many of their families might be doing at this hour. This too was shown on national TV. Then David and Jonathan brought in a bucket of coal and we started the fire (the wood

is used to start the fire and then the coal is added), and then we continued to talk Mongolia.

It must have been a good interview for it was almost impossible for us to get on a city bus during the next few weeks without somebody pointing to us with a big smile and

saying "Oh, I saw you on TV. You're the American who lives in a ger." By then my Mongolian was improving and I could converse a bit and say things such as, we liked Mongolia, we liked horses, we liked living in a ger and we thought that Mongols were great people.

One last thing about gers. They throw a rope over the top of the ger and tie one end to an old car engine and the other end to a bit of a tree trunk or something else. You see in the U.S. when the wind reaches seventy-five miles an hour they call it a hurricane, but in Mongolia they simply call it spring, and gers have been known to blow away. The wind comes down from the North Pole right through Siberia and there is nothing to stop it before it hits Mongolia at a gale force.

Laura in her kitchen. Notice doorway to the 2nd ger.

CHAPTER 14

1996: An Election & The New Testament

"In the sight of Him whom Abraham believed, even God,
who calls into being that which does not exist."
Romans 4:17

In April of 1996, the upcoming U.S. Presidential election already dominated the news in the United States even though the election was still more than half a year away. However, in that same spring of 1996 with the entire Mongolian Parliament up for election in just ten weeks, not a word was being said about the election. The Mongol people didn't really know yet how democracy worked. How could they? They had been raised on Communism and though they were technically democratic, the people themselves really knew very little about the electoral process.

The Mongolian Parliament had seventy-five members, seventy-two were of the Communist Party and only three were Democrats. Up and down the hallways of government buildings at two o'clock in the afternoon sat empty whisky and vodka bottles whose contents had just recently been consumed. Something had to be done. What were the chances of the Democrats winning the election?

When I asked Mongols about the chances of whether the Democrats could win the election they literally laughed out loud. The believers smiled politely, but they shook their head and said, "None." NONE? That was unacceptable. Things were falling apart. Things needed to change. Politically, Mongolia was a mess. But most Mongols didn't believe that the Democrats had a chance. I looked out the window and on the street people were standing at the bus stop waiting for the bus. Nothing was happening. No posters were up. No hand bills being handed out. No one was talking.

There were then ten weeks before the election as I began making phone calls to pull together the first prayer meeting for the election, which was to be held that coming Sunday evening. It didn't matter if only five people showed up, I knew the Lord wanted me there, and that He wanted the Church to begin to pray for the coming election.

The word was circulated to as many churches as could be contacted on such short notice that a prayer meeting for the coming election was taking place that Sunday evening. The worship team of one of the churches came to start things off with some praise songs. Around seventy-five people came.

The spirit was intense and the prayers were fervent. It was announced that the prayer meeting would be held every Sunday evening until the election, and for everyone to spread the word. The second meeting had over a hundred people in attendance and the third 125, 150, 180 and then over 200 as many people began to respond to the message being preached at the prayer meetings.

Before the prayer meetings started happening, it was obvious the main problem was that no one had any faith that things could change. The Communist system they had grown up under taught them to just accept things the way they were, and to be glad for what they had, even if it was nothing, because there wasn't anything that could be done. Obviously the thing that was needed was faith that things could change. Romans 4:17 says the God of Abraham "calls into being those things which do not exist." What did not exist was faith, and so we asked the Lord for faith for the Mongol people to believe that things could change, and the people began to believe. "How much faith do we need?" I cried, and we read from Mark 4:31 that, "it only takes a little faith, just the size of a mustard seed, and God can do great things." And week, by week, faith began to grow.

The church in Erdenet wanted to hear this message and invited me to their church. I asked, "What did Jesus say to the disciples in the boat? He said, 'Let's go to the other side.' There are no jobs on this side. Let's go to the other side. There's no food on this side, there's no telephones, no electricity, no purpose, no vision. Let's go to the other side. You can make a difference. You can choose the way your country will go. Let's go to the other side." I was preaching at the top of my lungs and the congregation in Erdenet just exploded. You could almost see their faith growing that things could change.

Back in Ulaanbaatar the following week, the church began to understand that God's desire was to use them to speak to their countrymen that things could change. "God wants to use the Christians of this country to speak to the nation, but you have to have faith and believe. You need to talk to your neighbors, talk to your friends. You have to help them understand that you have the power to change things." The church began praying with all of their heart at the meetings. They prayed and prayed and prayed, and things began to change! The atmosphere in the meetings moved from one of doubt, to one of faith and hope. People began talking to other people about the election. It was wonderful.

By the seventh meeting in early June, two hundred and twenty-five people were attending the meetings from practically every church in the city. We prayed in small groups, we prayed one at a time, we prayed as a whole, and we prayed out loud all at the same time as the Koreans do. The microphone was opened at the end of one meeting and the meeting lasted another two hours as one person after another person after another came to testify to the faith that was being born in their hearts and to pray for their nation.

At the ninth prayer meeting in mid-June we met out by the Tol River where many of them had been baptized. There we sang, praising and worshipping the Lord, and the word about faith was preached, and once again we prayed. As the election would be the following Sunday, the suggestion came at the close of the meeting that we hold next week's meeting on Saturday night before the election and everyone eagerly agreed. Then someone asked what about moving the meeting to Sukhebaatar Square in front of the Parliament building in the center of town where the democratic revolution had taken place six years earlier, and now everyone got excited. There would be no guitars, we didn't want to cause a scene. We simply wanted to come and to pray and everyone liked the idea.

The following week at seven o'clock in the evening we gathered at Sukhebaatar Square and it was pouring rain. But that was no problem for we had been praying for rain too, and we took this as an answer to prayer. So we huddled back under the eves of the surrounding government buildings and waited. About forty-five minutes later, the storm, that had displayed wonderful lightning, had passed, and the rain stopped, and we came out onto the large square in the center of Ulaanbaatar. We walked and we talked and then we looked up and saw it.

The sun was setting in the west and the storm was moving off to the east, and there right over our heads was as big and beautiful a rainbow as you would ever hope to see. Faith? There was no doubt in anyone's mind as to where that rainbow had come from and Who put it there. And so our conversation turned to shouts of joy, and we laughed and prayed, and thanked the Lord for the rain, for His grace, His goodness, His love... and His rainbow.

The new Eagle TV station with Christian backing from America had aired many advertisements on behalf of the democratic candidates, and the newspapers were now predicting that the Democrats might pick up twelve to fifteen seats in the election. No one had any idea what was going to happen in the election but I knew we had done everything we could to bring faith to the church and we all went home that Saturday evening at peace. After all, there was that rainbow.

On Sunday everyone went to church and several people talked about the meeting the night before, about the rainbow, and were urging everyone to be sure and vote that afternoon. It was nice to see the excitement and the hope the church now had. Different ones testified of how they had been witnessing to their neighbors the last few weeks, saying that in a democracy they had the power to change things. Well the church definitely had a new understanding as to how democracy worked, mainly by communicating and talking to one another and to their neighbors. It had been a good campaign.

That afternoon the nation voted and the next morning Mongolia awoke to the news that they had made headlines around the world. The Democrats had taken fifty of the seventy-five seats in Parliament! It was a miracle! An absolute miracle! A wave of euphoria swept the nation! Victory! It was joy unspeakable and full of glory! Of course everyone was putting their own spin on what happened, but as the pre-election polls were predicting the Democrats to gain only twelve to fifteen seats, there had to be another explanation. As for the Church, we knew that the Lord had responded to the cries of His people and had answered our prayers. It wasn't too different from when the Berlin Wall came down in response to the Church in Europe standing together and being the salt and light it is supposed to be. It doesn't happen that dramatically very often, but when it does... behold how good and how pleasant it is when the Church comes together in unity and prays. And so the Lord commanded a blessing.

That year of 1996 turned out to be a big one for the Mongols as the Mongolian Bible Translation Committee of which I had become the director, published the New Testament. Boldbaatar who was the primary translator was aided by a dedicated Korean woman named Sara Lee who translated 1, 2 and 3 John, and then by a number of Mongols and missionaries who helped in checking the manuscripts. The work went through numerous checks back and forth from Mongols to missionaries to Mongols, and so forth. Finally a Mongolian linguist named Tserenpil who had become a believer also helped in editing the manuscripts.

Boldbaatar

Boldbaatar had worked day and night and had really poured himself into the work. He had a burden. He knew the Mongolian people needed the word of God.

Another one of the people who helped check the manuscripts was a famous Mongolian poet named Orianhai who had become a believer. As Orianhai was quite a bit older, he added a certain quality to the translation, as he knew older words that greatly enriched the text.

By mid-September, Bold had finished the revisions, and the text of the twenty-seven books of the New Testament were ready for proof-reading. The manuscripts had now been through six checks by both missionaries and Mongols, and this would be the seventh. Some of the Mongols who had questioned what we were doing when we had begun two years earlier now helped in checking the final text. It had not been easy getting to this point, fighting the devil tooth and nail every day, and I wondered what would happen as we gathered together to proof-read the whole manuscript?

We had two monitors hooked up to a computer and there were four Mongolians all looking at the same text on the monitors. Boldbaatar and a couple of other men would then read the text out loud as everybody looked on together. In this way we had at least seven pair of eyes all checking the same text, at the same time, and if a change needed to be made, we did it there on the spot. And then a strange and wonderful thing happened.

It was as if the Lord placed a hedge around us as we worked together. We would all be in the office reading the texts and it seemed like we were in the hollow of God's hand. Total chaos could be going on outside (and often was), but in that room we felt as though the *Shikina* glory of God was upon us. We would begin work at nine o'clock in the morning and work until one o'clock in the afternoon. This was four hours of very arduous, intense labor, but instead of feeling drained, everyone would finish feeling refreshed. We usually ate lunch together and sometimes people would stay on and discuss the texts, or simply to remain in the warm atmosphere that had come upon us. As we parted we truly looked forward to getting together the next morning. It was a special time we will always remember. After the extensive process we had been through and the opposition we'd endured from the translator of the Bible Society for using traditional Mongolian terminology it was as if the Lord said, "Enough," and the enemy could do us no more harm.

An amazing man named John Thompson now comes into our story in an interesting way. John was a Scotsman who had come as a missionary to Mongolia back in 1992, and had since gone to work for the United Nations Children's Fund, UNICEF. John Thompson was tall, his hair usually disheveled, and was one of those people that are rightfully called geniuses. He was way, way ahead of everyone else in the country regarding computers, and when we needed anything fixed pertaining to any of our computers, John never hesitated in coming right over. He took care of every problem, no matter what it was, hardware or software, it didn't matter, John Thompson could fix it. Here was this guy giving his life to serve Christ in outer Mongolia, who could easily have been making six figures a year back in the West.

John was also helping us format the text as we went along and monitored our progress closely during the proofreading, until finally the day came when we were finished, all the checking was complete, and no more changes would be made. I was really busy with a lot of different things at this time, overseeing Basan and Bayarsaihan on the trains, helping lead the International Church, taking care of our kindergartens, and itinerating around the Mongol churches, so I had a lot of irons in the fire, and when John Thompson called me the night we finished, the import of what he said didn't really register with me. In fact, it was two o'clock the following afternoon when it finally dawned on me just what he had said. I picked up the phone and dialed his number. "Hello, John, ah, last night on the phone, ah, did you say you had made a *concordance* from our New Testament?"

"That's right. It's 335 pages long if you would like to see it."

I could hardly believe my ears (Geniuses! Wow!). "Actually John, I don't think we can use the whole thing, but if you would allow us to use part of it, we'd be glad to put twenty-five pages of selected words in the back of the book." "Oh that's no problem," John said in his beautiful Scottish lilt. "That's what it's for."

What a guy! But then an odd thing happened as John's wife became dangerously ill, and they had to leave for the UK immediately. It was very serious because before any of us knew it, they were gone. I never saw John Thompson again, but in the midst of their exit, he sent us a disc with instructions for the concordance.

My coworker on the Mongolian Bible Translation Committee (MBTC) was Takashi, and together we began printing out the manuscript on a laser printer in order to send it to the publisher. We were just hours away from sending the manuscript off when we put the floppy disc John Thompson had left into the computer. Takashi opened the file and the screen looked like a snowfall of hieroglyphics. Good grief.

Then Takashi re-read the directions out loud. Do this, do this, do this, ah, we hadn't done that, do this, do this… hit enter… and…BINGO, there it was, twenty-five pages of concordance *perfectly formatted* and ready for the printer. When Takashi pushed the last command, it was like a miracle, as the hieroglyphics turned into the Mongolian script and everything was there. Takashi and I literally shouted for joy. Amazing! How had John Thompson done it?

Takashi added a short two-page glossary of key terms to put in the back, and off we sent the manuscript to Japan for printing and waited for its return. A big question still to come would be getting the books through Mongolian customs. There was nothing illegal in importing books, but you never knew what customs might do.

In late November, the books arrived and somehow the word "Bibles" got mentioned at the customs office and red flags went up. A customs official was sent out to the container with the New Testaments. The container was opened, revealing hundreds and hundreds of boxes containing the newly printed New Testaments. The customs official who was there opened up one of the boxes, took out a New Testament, read a few lines, looked at his coworker and said "*Zaa*," meaning *okay*. The tax was paid and the shipment of ten thousand New Testaments was secured as we unloaded the boxes onto the back of a five-ton truck.

The books started selling rapidly, and by Christmas all ten thousand books had been sold! Incredible! It was as if the church was proving that man does not live by bread alone, but by every word that proceeds from the mouth of God. Plans were immediately made for a second printing of eight thousand more New Testaments.

In the months that followed the publishing of the New Testament, it wasn't long before one Mongolian church leader after another began using the traditional Mongolian word, *Burkhan*, instead of 'Master of the Universe.' It was as if all they needed was permission. Within six months, the translation done by the MBTC had become the standard Bible used by the believers in Mongolia. Soon ninety-eight percent of the Body of Christ was using the new translation. I had been correct in my belief that if given a choice the Mongols would choose their own traditional terms.

It was the Mongol believers who were to confirm for many of the missionaries that *Burkhan* was indeed the name of the Creator in their language, and that *Burkhan* did not mean Buddha. All Mongols knew that Buddha was simply called "the teacher of *Burkhan*," and was not *Burkhan* Himself. And so it was by virtue of the Mongol believers own choosing that traditional Mongolian words became the standard terminology in the churches.

The Church continued to grow and celebrate new life in Christ.

CHAPTER 15

Hamágui, Spritual Warfare & Fasting

"And the serpent said to the woman, 'You surely will not die.'"
Genesis 3:4

When we'd arrived in Mongolia back in 1992, everyone was talking about something called the Year of the Monkey. The Buddhist calendar is built around a twelve year cycle, with each year bearing the name of some animal such as tiger, elephant, mouse, etc. The Year of the Monkey is supposed to be the coldest year of the twelve year cycle so that many more animals and people than normal are expected to die. As unscientific and thus unbelievable as this is to people in the West, in Mongolia it was front page news! It was on the radio daily, the television, and on everybody's mind and lips. Everywhere you went people were whispering about the Year of the Monkey and genuine fear was in their conversation. The odd thing was that at this point it had been an unusually cool summer and it was now cold in mid-September. Then I was invited by Basanhu to teach a Wednesday evening Bible study at the Fellowship Church.

"Let's turn in our Bibles to Acts chapter one and verse seven," I said, after greeting the congregation of about forty that evening. "Now I have been hearing a lot about the Year of the Monkey this week," I began and you could have heard a pin drop. It was not *good luck* to speak so openly about this, but of course, depending on *luck* was one of the things I was wanting to challenge. "Now verse seven says that the times and the seasons are in the hands of our Father. I have heard that the Year of the Monkey is supposed to be the coldest year of the Buddhist calendar. Is that right?" I asked. A few heads nodded but most people were really wide-eyed that I was talking about this. Superstition in Mongolia, as I was to learn more than once, runs deep.

"Now we all know that if it is a cold winter this year in Mongolia that it is going to reinforce the Mongol people's belief in Buddhism." Now I had everybody's attention. "Do you think that we could ask our Father in whose hands are the seasons to warm the weather up?"

Everyone was looking at me and finally someone said, "You're the missionary, you tell us."

"Oh but it doesn't matter what I say, I am a man just like you. What matters is what God says." Now that put things in a different light. So I said, "Let's read the verse again," and we did. And then I said, "What do you think? Do you think we can pray and ask the Lord to warm the weather up?" Now many heads began to nod as the word of God started to grip their hearts. "Okay, let's pray," I said, and we divided into small groups and we began to pray. When we came back together I continued to teach from Acts 1, and we had a good study together, but the best was yet to come. An hour later when we walked outside, the weather was noticeably warmer!

This was an encouraging sign but I sensed that much more was at stake here and so I wrote a prayer letter from Mongolia to all of our supporters and entitled it, "Mongolia and the Year of the Monkey", explaining how serious the ramifications of the situation would be if it were a cold winter and told our supporters to pray and ask God to bring a warm winter to Mongolia. The letter went out in late September, and was received by our prayer supporters around October 3, and suddenly the weather got warmer in Mongolia.

And the weather remained warm throughout October, and was warm in November, as we enjoyed a beautiful Indian summer. But then, December stayed warm too! Wow! The weather didn't turn cold until Jan. 6, and stayed cold for only three weeks. Then on Jan. 26, the weather warmed up again! After that I looked out of our apartment window each morning and saw the smoke coming from the stacks at the power plant on the west side of the city, and EVERY day, it showed the wind was blowing from the south. I would walk out the door of the building an hour later and would literally burst out in praise to the Lord praying, "Melt it down Lord, melt it down!" By mid-February there was no snow on the ground anywhere in Ulaanbaatar, and by the end of February there was no snow in the surrounding mountains, and Mongolia had just recorded its warmest winter on record, fifteen degrees above normal! Now that was an answer to prayer.

But a strange thing about human nature though is that these kind of inconsistencies tend to get overlooked, and so it was in Mongolia. Had the winter been cold? Had more animals and people died than normal? Nobody was talking about the fact that the Year of the Monkey had not been cold, but warm, and so I wrote an article calling people's attention to the warm winter just experienced in the Year of the Monkey, and took it to a local newspaper. As the Mongolian editor looked over my article, a wry smile came to his face as he recognized the things I was pointing out were true, and agreed to print the article in his newspaper, which he did.

Five years later the big news as the calendar turned to 1997, was that a total eclipse of the sun would take place in Mongolia in March. In Ulaanbaatar the eclipse was supposed to reach 99.6%, while in Darhan and Erdenet it would be 100%. We had no idea the surprise that was waiting for us.

The word on the street was that celebrities like Madonna, Stevie Wonder, and others were coming to view the eclipse. Special cups and mugs were being sold in the department store as Mongols were learning how to market events like the eclipse.

On the morning of the eclipse we got our kids up to go outside and look at the eclipse. But we found Ulaanbaatar was like a ghost town. The streets were totally empty! It was 8 a.m. but there were no people on the streets! It was incredible. There were no buses running, no policemen out, no taxis, nothing. What was going on?

At that time Ulaanbaatar was a city of 800,000 people, and yet extraordinarily no one was out of doors. The reason? The shamans and Buddhist lamas had told everyone the age-old explanation, "that a dragon was eating the sun, and no one was to go outside." Incredibly they had instilled such fear in the minds of the nation through their long-held tradition about eclipses that no one dared challenge what they said. Though this was nothing but superstition, it let us see just how strong a hold it still had on the Mongolian people. Witchcraft was alive and well in Mongolia.

There was no one on the streets. Even educated people, college professors, government officials, scholars, scientists, and the like. All believed to some degree the official line of the shamans and lamas. People didn't follow through with common sense and ask the telling question of "why?" If a dragon had eaten the sun, why in just a few hours was it out shining again? The fact was superstition and spiritual blindness still held these people in bondage to a far greater degree than we had imagined. It's amazing how Satan can blind the minds of people, and keep the simplest inconsistencies from being seen.

A young Mongolian man once asked me, "Are you a materialist, a dualist, or an idealist?" I couldn't help but think back to the time when the old herdsman who gave Jessica the lamb, came up to me and said, "I'm not a Buddhist, and I'm not a Communist," then asked, "What do you have to tell me?" Essentially these two men had asked the same question, only in different ways. At the heart of both of their inquiries lay the underlying question, "What is truth?"

The Roman governor Pontius Pilate asked Jesus Christ, "What is truth?" Along with love, this is the message that Christians have to share with the world. Pilate asked Jesus, "Are you a king?"

"My kingdom is not of this world," Jesus replied. Here was the truth standing right in front of him but Pilate couldn't see it. Had a dragon eaten the sun? Had the Year of the Monkey been the coldest winter? No, but perplexingly, no one seemed to question the facts. Jesus said, "You shall know the truth and the truth shall set you free."

As Jesus told Pilate, "My kingdom is not of this world," He gives us an insight into ultimate truth. This world is not all that there is. This earth is not our home, though secular humanists would like us to believe otherwise. What does truth bring? Truth brings hope. There is another world. Jesus came into this world, from another world, and whoever will believe in Him will not perish but will go to live in that other world. Here is truth, and it brings hope beyond all superstition. The eclipse itself was fantastic. When you know the truth, you are free to appreciate the wonders of the universe.

It wasn't long after we had arrived in Mongolia that my wife and I began to notice an aspect of the culture, which in Mongolian is called *hamágui*. In the Mongolian language the word *hamaa* means "to matter" and the suffix *gui* negates things, so that *hamágui* literally means, *it doesn't matter,* and we would hear it everyday over and over again. Nevertheless *hamágui* is a lie. Things do matter. People matter. God matters. And His word matters. I began to see and understand *hamágui* in a spiritual way, a spirit that goes all the way back to the Garden of Eden where Satan essentially said, 'it doesn't matter what God says.' Furthermore it seemed as if *hamágui* had found ready rails to run on via Communism. As a result the people were in bondage to this spirit. Many times we saw children standing outside the buildings where they lived throwing whisky bottles, vodka bottles, beer bottles, or any other kind of bottle up against the building just to see them shatter.

But the even greater tragedy was that the children's parents were standing nearby. None of them bothered to stop them or say a word of reproof. *Hamágui.* It doesn't matter. The city was covered in broken glass, which was pretty symbolic of the way things were, and the attitude was *hamágui.*

Here was a whole way of thinking that needed to change. How to turn such a mindset around? When dealing with parts of a culture's worldview which are not of God, and which need to be changed, we must turn once again to the well known passage from Ephesians 6:12 that tells us, "We do not wrestle/war/fight against flesh and blood, but with powers and principalities, against the world forces of darkness, against spiritual wickedness in high places." And this is where we began to fight.

In Ephesians 4:11-12, Paul writes that Christ gave the church "apostles, prophets, evangelists, pastors and teachers, to equip the saints for the work of the ministry." But what is this work of the ministry? Is it just the explanation of the gospel? Or is there more involved than just explanation? In Genesis 3, after the fall of Adam and Eve, God spoke to the serpent who had just committed the first terrorist attack in world history, and said, "Cursed are you, on your belly shall you go and dust shall you eat, all the days of your life… and I will put enmity between your seed, and the seed of the woman… He will crush your head, and you will bruise his heel" (Gen. 3:14-15).

Have no doubt about it, when God speaks about crushing the devil's head, He is talking war. And here we see something rather profound about God. Ironically, we see just how much He really loves us, for His love is so great that He is willing to go to war. And with this first prophecy, God was surely making an announcement, not only to the serpent, but also to the powers and principalities of darkness looking on, and to all of posterity, which would include you and me. And basically His announcement was to mark His words, there was going to be a rescue operation on Planet Earth!

And this rescue operation has been the primary agenda of God from that moment when He spoke the prophecy until now as you read this page. If you are saved, then you have been rescued, and are one of the saints in Eph. 4:12. As we read the verse it is plain that God now wants those who have been rescued to be equipped to work together with Him in the rescue operation. This is the work of the ministry which Paul speaks of in this passage. This rescue operation involves toil and struggle against the powers and principalities of darkness. There is a war going on, a very real conflict between kingdoms, and God calls all of His people to participate. The spread of the gospel is not just an educational process of proclamation, but also a spiritual war in which we must engage. *Hamágu* cannot be part of our thinking. Everything matters.

Satan constantly tries to get us to criticize others, speak negatively, and complain about everything. We must discipline ourselves to learn to speak positively to win the battle. When I was a first-term missionary in the Philippines and whining about the culture, I wrote a letter to our friend and author Miriam Adney complaining, "Why can't they pick up their garbage? They pile their garbage ten feet high at the end of the street? What a place!" Miriam very astutely wrote back saying, "Well Rick, as I recall you were pretty critical of American culture when you were here." Oh did that ever hit home. What an eye opening 'Aha' moment her statement produced for me. We must set aside our critical spirits and look past the garbage to the lost humanity held in bondage all around us whether we are in the United States or on a mission field. We must take every thought captive.

In the last days of August in 1997, the Mongol church leaders came together for three days of fasting and prayer. They went outside of Ulaanbaatar about an hour's drive to a spot along the Tol River and camped out in tents. A big cross, perhaps twelve feet high, was erected at the place where we came together for morning, afternoon, and evening times of corporate prayer.

Fasting is something that draws believers closer to God. The fast was scheduled for three days, and it is usually the second day of a fast that is the hardest. But then there is a breakthrough on the third day, and in fact if one is fasting for a week, days three to seven are usually filled with peace and blessing, as one begins to physically not live by bread alone.

There were a couple of pages of song sheets so that everyone could sing together, and each morning and evening we came together to worship the Lord. That first evening everyone scattered out to gather firewood for the evening. There was also plenty of time just to wait on God. As there is a great deal of misunderstanding about what it means to "wait upon the Lord" I gave a short teaching on the subject.

In Hebrew, the word "wait" literally means "to twist together," as in making a rope. So for example the meaning of the passage from Isaiah 40:31, "They that wait upon the Lord shall renew their strength," literally comes out, "They that twist their wills together with God's will, shall find their strength renewed." This transforms "waiting" from a passive to an active role, seeking to be engaged with God's will. With a greater understanding and motivation as to what it is to "wait" on the Lord, we corporately sought to twist our wills together with His.

As these were the last days of August, we had the entire National Park to ourselves. Vacations were over and schools had started again. But the weather was still warm though the leaves were turning their beautiful fall yellows, and the river was clear and not so swift as it is in the spring. Everyone found it good to come away from the mad rush of ministry in which we were all involved, simply enjoying the Lord and spending time together in the fellowship of His Spirit. More than seventy people had come together to fast and pray.

As the church in Erdenet turned five years old, they held a celebration to praise the Lord for what He had done in their midst. The church had been officially turned over to the Mongolian leadership after three years with a formal ceremony "passing the baton" from the missionaries to the

Mongols. There were by now over seven hundred people in more than fifty cell groups. Therefore the church needed to rent the largest hall in Erdenet, which seated nine hundred for the event. Many people from Ulaanbaatar had taken the train up to celebrate with the church, and as the worship began, it was standing room only, with both aisles along the sides of the auditorium filled, as more than a thousand people gathered in Jesus' name.

By this time the worship team in Erdenet was a seasoned group and knew how to keep their focus on Jesus, and the Holy Spirit came upon us as we lifted our hands and our hearts to honor the Lord for all that He had done in only five years! What a work the Lord was doing in this place.

The church had now started what was called the MMC, which stood for, Mongolian Mission Center, and the church began training, and sending church planting teams all over Mongolia and beyond. The Mongols who came for training were like the apostle Paul who said in Philippians 3:12, "I press on to take hold of *that* for which Christ Jesus took hold of me." There is a profound beauty to the small pronoun, "that".

What is, "that?" Whatever else we do in life, we must not miss "that." For if we miss "that" we miss what we have been created for. "That" will change from time to time in our lives. For now, "that" meant being at the training center, and it was important that the students lay hold of all that the Lord has for them there. It's like getting married. What people must do is focus in on the Lord and His purpose for their life and He will bring them and their mate together in His perfect timing. "I know the plans I have for you," says the Lord, "plans that are good and not of calamity, to give you a future and a hope" (Jer. 29:11).

When Jesus was on his way to Jerusalem as recorded in Mark 11, He sent two of His disciples to get a little donkey for Him to sit on. "We are that little donkey," I shared with the students. "Take a look at this little donkey at the beginning of the story. There he is, tied up, standing on the street with nothing to do, probably bored to tears. Many people in the world fit this description. No one likes to be bored. And then one day, someone comes along and tells you about Jesus, unties you, and brings you to Christ. Here we have a picture of salvation.

"But before Jesus can ride this little donkey, something else needs to happen. That little donkey has to be equipped. And so we see the people putting their garments on the donkey and here we have a picture of discipleship. If you are going to carry the King, you have to become equipped; you have to be prepared. Now if the little donkey jumps around and refuses to stand still so that he can be equipped, if he doesn't come to class and skips Bible study or the prayer meeting, what happens? The donkey doesn't get to carry the King.

"However if the little donkey allows himself to be equipped, look what happens to him. Suddenly his life is transformed from dull and boring, standing around with nothing to do, to being right in the middle of the greatest celebration on Planet Earth with people laying palm branches at his feet and providing his every need. But most important of all, he has the privilege of carrying the King."

The church at Khara Khorum

And this is what the MMC began to do. They soon were "carrying the King," training and sending church planting teams ALL OVER Mongolia! These young people sent out from the MMC in Erdenet came to sacrifically serve the Lord in some very difficult places. The local authorities where they went were absolutely amazed at how these young Mongolian Christians came to serve their fellow Mongols in their adopted communities. And so the Lord blessed the work of their hands and the love in their hearts and churches were planted from Khara Khorum to Khuvsgul, and on and on and on.

A key principle they learned at the MMC and which we all need to learn is from 1 Cor. 9:20-22, "To the Jews I became like a Jew, to win the Jews. To those under the law I became like one under the law (though I myself am not under the law), so as to win those under the law… to the weak, I became weak, to win the weak. I have become all things to all men so that by all possible means I might save some." Here is the principle of overcoming one's own self-centeredness in order to identify, and become accepted by those whom you have come to reach. In this passage from 1 Cor. 9:20-22, the focus is on contextualizing the messenger. However in Matthew 5:17, we see Jesus focusing on contextualizing the message to the culture itself.

After finishing the Beatitudes, (Matt. 5:3-16), Jesus said, "Do not think that I came to abolish the Law and the Prophets (the foundation of Jewish religion and culture), I did not come to abolish, but to fulfill." And so it is with every culture. Of all the verses in the Bible, surely this is one of the most important for a missionary. It is God Himself who made the different cultures of the world, and therefore the Son of God does not come to abolish them, but to fulfill them. Cultures add beauty and richness to life, as well as the breadth of understanding of what is going on in the world.

For example, in Mongolia there is *Tsagaan Sar* which we have already noted. So exquisite and beautiful a celebration in the morning, like the very wholesomeness which God intended when He created the world, only to end up by evening corrupted by Satan, in a drunken stupor. When teaching this in Mongolian churches, I would use the illustration of an inebriated Uncle Baatar, passed out with his face in the potato salad, and let my head fall forward onto the pulpit as if I were Uncle Baatar. Everyone would roar with laughter as they had all seen something like this many times over the years. It was an object lesson, which was instantly recognizable, and easily connected with the people.

"But rather than abolishing *Tsagaan Sar*, what would happen if we allow Jesus to touch *Tsagaan Sar* by bringing God's law into *Tsagaan Sar* that says do not get drunk? *Tsagaan Sar* would then be transformed, fulfilled, so that it is as beautiful in the evening as it was in the morning," and the people would all nod their heads in agreement. Jesus doesn't come to abolish, but to fulfill.

Take the Mongol's tradition during the morning milking. Today, as you read this page, literally thousands of mothers, daughters, and grandmothers, milked their family's cow or goat, to provide for their family's staple nourishment of milk tea, and as they did this, they threw a cup of milk in the air as an offering to God. Is this wrong? How should a missionary respond to this? Should he try to stop it? No. This is not wrong. It is merely a form of worship. The question the missionary should ask is, "To whom are you throwing the milk?" It is not the missionary's role to question whether throwing milk is a legitimate form of worship (simply because it is different from his own), but his attention should be directed to the content of the worship, not the form. Jesus said, "An hour is coming when the true worshippers will worship the Father in spirit and in truth, for such people the Father seeks to be his worshippers" (John 4:23).

Missionaries and Christians in general, must be willing to accept different forms. "Neither in his mountain, nor in Jerusalem. . . . but in spirit and in truth." God does not expect everyone around the world to worship Him in exactly the same way. Jesus does not come to abolish the cultures of the world, but to fulfill them.

When the little old ladies heard the teaching about milking one's cow, which they do every day of the year, they were overjoyed. They rushed forward at the close of the meeting saying thank you, thank you. God loves them just the way they were, and they could worship God just the way they had been doing since they were little girls, only now with greater and more fulfilled meaning. This message based on the crucial principle called contextualization, had really spoken to their hearts. The more common ground that can be found and redeemed, the greater the opportunity for communicating truth, so that more people can understand the message.

The Mongols loved stories and as wrestling was their national sport the message from Genesis 32 where the angel of the Lord wrestled with Jacob to let go of his fear was a great story to tell. The Mongolian people could easily identify with and understand wrestling as a metaphor, espe-

cially when related to wrestling with fear as Jacob had done in Genesis 32. As Basan listened to this teaching he then offered that Jacob's crossing over the Jabbok River the following day was like Jacob's baptism. I'd never thought of that. How amazing the insight and understanding people can gain from God's word.

However cross-cultural communication was not always so clear. One day I was sitting with Basan and I wanted to talk to him about spiritual warfare. So I thought I would try to catch him by surprise and to get his attention I began, "You know, Basan, I really like to fight." Basan practically jumped out of his chair, "So do I!" he exclaimed. I couldn't help laughing as I had never seen him so animated. "No, no, no, I am not talking about fist fighting. I am talking about fighting the devil."

CHAPTER 16

Starfish, Street Kids, & Aase

"I tell you the truth,
whatever you did for one of the least of these brothers of mine,
you did for me."
Matt. 25:30

One Sunday evening at the International Church, one of the long-standing missionaries from Germany stood to her feet with a testimony that would change many of our lives. She said the day before she had been waiting to catch a bus, and there was this little boy next to her all covered in dirt. "Where do you live?" she asked.

"Right there," came the reply.

Looking around and seeing nothing she said, "Right where?"

"Right there," and this time the little boy pointed to the man hole they were standing beside.

With eyes wide, the German woman asked, "May I see?"

"Sure," said the boy, and down they went. It turned out there were thousands of kids living in the tunnels under the city where the heating ducts passed. Thousands. We sat like statues, absolutely stunned as she told us the story. What could be done?

A few weeks later I was down at the train station putting someone on the train to Erdenet, and when I turned around, there were a couple of these street kids who were covered with soot from head to foot from the coal that ran the trains, wrestling and throwing each other on the platform. And the Lord said, "I want you to help these kids." Boy my heart sure went out to these little guys. The question was, "What was the best way to help?"

The principle the Lord had given me since the first time I came to Mongolia was "love never fails" and so it seemed to me that the thing these kids needed more than anything was love. I remembered something I had heard growing up was that you can give a baby everything it needs, but if you don't give it love, it will die.

I was also aware that most Mongol believers were in need of meaningful employment. Could providing foster care become a double blessing for the church? I approached several couples about taking street children into their homes as a ministry, offering to provide for the children's physical needs, as well as giving the couple a salary, if they would take care of them. But at first, no one responded positively. Had I misunderstood God's direction or had I just not found the ones He would had call for the task. After all, these were street kids and they made a living by stealing.

Then I met Bilgee and his wife Boynaa, a young couple from the town of Gobi-Altai who had two little girls. They had brought their ger with them and were living on the side of a hill out in what was called the Third Micro District.

We sat down and explained to Bilgee and Boynaa what we had in mind and that we would supply all of the boy's physical needs and bear all their expenses, but it was up to them to provide the most important element of love. Not only did Bilgee and Boynaa understand what we were saying, but they totally agreed, as they had met the Lord themselves some 4 years before. Bilgee helped lead worship in his church and looked like a young man with a lot of promise, but it was Boynaa who convinced me that they were the right people for the job, as she was the epitome of a mother hen! It would take a special ability to work with street children, and Bilgee and Boynaa had the gift.

It was January and the temperature was about thirty below zero when we went down to the police station where they kept the runaways and street children. There were forty to fifty of them running around buck naked, skinny as a rail, with shaved heads. Boynaa wanted to take them all. "No, no, no," I said, "we can't take them all." But Boynaa's mothering instinct was in high gear. I suggested we take eight or nine, but one look at the hurt in Boynaa's eyes and I knew that was out of the question. "Ok, what if we take twelve," but still she wasn't satisfied. I think we finally came home with fifteen boys, aged five to sixteen.

They all slept that night in Bilgee and Boynaa's ger, and tomorrow we would start digging into the side of the mountain to lay the floor for what would be the boy's ger. The next day we began hacking and chipping away into the hillside of rock and frozen earth to level out a place for the floor. We worked together for six or seven hours and got about half done. The angle of the ground in Bilgee's *hashaa* was close to forty-five degrees, which did not make things easy. By the time we had finished digging, the bank on the uphill side was close to four feet high! The third day we set up the ger, put in the stove, and the boys moved into their new home. Slugging away at laying that foundation had been a good time of bonding between Bilgee and me and the boys. Perhaps they saw we were willing to go the extra mile with them.

I wrote to our prayer supporters, "A young man walked along the seashore, throwing starfish back into the sea after a high tide had washed thousands of the helpless creatures up onto the shore. A bystander looking on deridingly asked, 'What do you think you are doing? Do you really think what you're doing makes any difference?' The young man bent down, picked up another starfish and threw it back into the water and said, 'It just made a difference for that one.' And so our ministry to these starfish, these street urchins had begun.

Next I made arrangements for all the boys to go to a special school set up by Korean missionaries who worked with the poor. But three days later I got a call from Bilgee saying the boys had all been expelled. What? I called the principal and he explained that he had already given the boys a second chance and that he had to enforce the rules or it would compromise the school. And so they were out. Their crime? Smoking… at nine years old! Good grief. What to do?

There was a new woman in Dambadarja across from our friends Basan and Sambo, who had moved in from the countryside, from out in western Mongolia, and she was supposed to be a teacher. I wondered if she would consider taking on our boys? Her name was Togtogbayar, and she said she would give working with the boys a try. Being from the countryside and coming from the west made Togtogbayar and her husband about as real a Mongol as one could get. Her father was a teacher and she had grown up with a good education and seemed to know just how to motivate the boys and inspire them towards learning.

So we created our own prep school to get the boys ready for real school. She had to teach them to obey rules, follow directions, keep to a schedule and other things which are normally taken for granted. But these kids had been living in the sewers for who knows how long, and they were not used to doing anything structured. But Togtogbayar was amazing, and the boys began to respond to her wise but gentle touch. As we got to know the boys more and more, their stories started to come out, sometimes through tears with tales that would break your heart… and sometimes chill your bones.

Little Bayanmonk was my favorite. He was a natural clown with a winning smile and a good voice. He had sung on the streets for the money to feed himself. How had he come to live on the streets? A few years back he was brought to Ulaanbaatar with his parents. They went to the Zax, which is the huge black market and somehow he got separated in the crowd and never saw his parents again. We had heard stories of parents who were so poor who thought they couldn't take care of their children, and would deliberately lose them at the market.

A few of the boys were true orphans without any parents, but most of the boys came from broken homes. A common scenario was that a boy's mother and father had separated, and then the mother had remarried to a man who would come home drunk and beat the boy's mother, and then beat the boy. Naturally it didn't take too many beatings before the kid decided to leave. Probably seventy percent of the kids on the street came from a background like that.

But now they were in a home where they were being cared for and loved in a way they had never known. Bilgee and Boynaa would take them to Sunday school which they took to like frosting on a donut, and soon they were singing about Jesus.

After three months of prep school the boys were ready to give the Korean school another try, and this time they made it. I had sat them down the weekend before the school began and just shared matter of factly that they couldn't do this, and they couldn't do that, and they seemed to understand. Togtogbayar had done her job well, and no doubt the Lord had His hand in there too.

Laura had begun to disciple Togtogbayar who had accepted the Lord after she had come to Ulaanbaatar. She had two boys of her own but during this time with our ex-street kids, whom we called the dirty dozen, she had a dream that she was taking care of little girls. She talked to Laura about the dream and asked if we would consider setting up a home for girls and let her take care of them. As Laura and I talked it over we both sensed this was the Lord, and so together with Togtogbayar we made another trip to the police station where they brought in kids from the street. There were two little girls who had just come in, one three years old, and the other five years old, and we took them both.

The five year-old said her mother brought her to the police station and told her to knock on the door. When she turned around her mother was gone. The policeman opened the door and there she was. That was

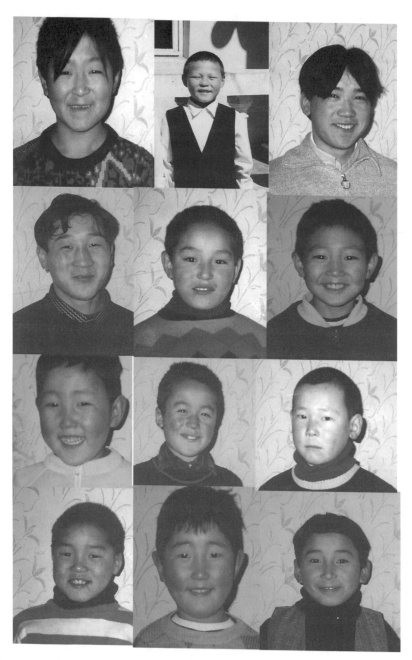

The Dirty Dozen

three weeks ago. The three year-old's mother was a totally irresponsible woman who could not take care of her child and likewise brought her to the police. A few weeks later the mother was begging us to also take her six year-old son, which we did. The change for these kids could only be rivaled by Joseph in the book of Genesis, going from a slave, to Prime Minister, as these little children suddenly found themselves in a home with a woman they would soon call mother, who would love them and take care of them.

The following Christmas, Togtogbatar invited us to her home for a meal and little party. So we bought some toys for the kids and off we went. When we arrived, there were a couple of Togtogbayar's relatives, a sister and a niece who had recently arrived in town. Her niece was sitting on the bed and didn't bother to get up (which was pretty unusual) when we came into the ger. The ger was fairly full with Laura and I, and our four children, Togtogbayar and her husband, their own two children and the three street children, plus her sister and niece. And then I happened to notice why the young fourteen year-old girl had not gotten up. She was missing a foot.

As you can imagine she was not a happy camper and looked pretty dejected as anyone might who at that young age had had their life permanently altered. I didn't try to make eye contact or draw her out at this time, but simply made sure she got a gift when they were handed out. The next day Toftogbayar came to our home and told us the story of the freak accident when a horse just six months before had crushed the foot so that it had to be removed. And now she was left with a crutch. But I knew with new prosthetic limbs that she could be helped, and so we made an appointment for the girl at Youngsei Hospital.

Dr. David Sir from Korea, who had founded the hospital, had been one of my closest friends in Mongolia. Together we started a couple of clinics in the ger districts as his staff would retrain Mongolian doctors in

Western medical practices. The medical practices we found in place when the country opened up back in 1990, included *bleeding* for headaches and the like, and much of the medical system was absolutely atrocious. Anyway, David let me bring in all my street children for free treatment plus any other medical emergency or need I came across. So Ornaa, which was the girl's name, was not the first patient I had brought to the hospital.

The people at the hospital treated Ornaa like a queen and I'll never forget her coming out of the hospital a few weeks later, after the prosthetic foot had been made for her and put on, a smile once again graced her countenance. There was new life, and hope for some kind of a future. Why, she might even grow up and get married!

Besides the street kids we took in, we also started a feeding program for the kids still out on the streets. I'd realized that there were essentially two kinds of kids on the streets, one was a sort of Huckleberry Finn who had probably run away from home, and though it was no doubt for good reasons, he was just playing around, living in the sewers, panhandling the tourists, and stealing anything he could get his hands on. The other kind of kid had a similar story, but deep down he would like to get off the street and go to school. I wanted to help them both so we took the kids in who were serious, and we provided meals for the ones who still needed some time to come to a point of wanting a change.

The younger the child when he or she came to us, the better the chance they had for staying. Some kids heard about our program and simply put us on the circuit of other organizations who were also helping street children. But Bilgee noticed the ones who came and stole and disappeared, and they were not allowed to return.

Samaritan's Purse heard of what we were doing and sent one of their representatives to check out our program. Evidently he liked what he saw because after that they would help with any needs the kids might have.

Another organization from Japan also took a special interest in our street kids and would annually have us over for a big Christmas party with all kinds of food to eat, plus games and presents for the kids. Being a fairly small organization, I was grateful for the greater body of Christ that was willing to work together with us in this way. I enjoyed working with the poor at the grass roots level. Often I picked up kids off the street and would take them out for a meal, find out a bit more about them and their needs, take them to the doctor, buy them a bag of groceries and talk to them a little about Jesus. Mongolia was simply a great place to be a missionary.

One of the workers who had joined us was a sixty-six year-old woman from Norway named Aase (pronounced OOSA). When I picked her up at the airport in Ulaanbaatar she had a backpack, a duffle bag, and one suitcase. Aase was an amazing woman, hardy, yet cultured, sophisticated, and very savvy to human nature. Aase turned out to be truly filled with the Holy Spirit and the love of God. She had been the national director of Women's Aglow in Norway. Now that her husband had passed on, she answered the Lord's call to come to Mongolia to disciple women and that is exactly what she did!

Aase could work with anyone because she did her work as unto the Lord, and so she moved easily through all social strata, able to work with those who were extremely poor, while at the same time knowing how to talk with high-ranking government officials. What a person was on the outside  made no difference to Aase. At her age, she well knew the only thing that matters is what is on the inside, and she was prepared to love everybody. Besides the Aglow fellowship, Aase had a vision for reaching women in prison, and the Lord gave her favor as no one else had been able to gain with prison officials. She was faithful, she was consistent, and she was loving, and love never fails. She could talk to a woman who had been in the Communist system all her life, and see her simply as a lost sister who needed to come to Christ, and she had the wisdom to be patient and win such a person a little at a time. Others before her had tried to go in and hit a home run when they stepped through the door, and were rebuffed and not invited back. But Aase abided in the Lord and therefore had a way about her that found favor in the eyes of the people she met, be they beggar or politician.

Aase discovered that a number of the women in the prison were gifted in the area of music, and was able to give them the opportunity for these talents to be expressed, so that one day she showed up at our door with an invitation to come to a special concert being put on by the women in the prison. The concert was at night and in a hall in town rather than out at the prison, which meant this was no small thing that Aase had been able to pull together. So Laura and I dressed up in our dells, picked Aase up along with the street children she was taking care of and whom she had basically adopted, (she had four girls and one boy), and headed off to the concert.

When we arrived, the parking lot was filling up, and many people from various walks of life were standing in the foyer when we entered. As was often the case in that kind of situation, we were not in control of things but simply had to let go and allow ourselves to be shown where they wanted us to sit and of course this was in the front row. I had learned long ago that in this situation it is best to come alive as everyone is watching, and it does no good to be a wallflower when you are on the front row, especially when it provides an excellent opportunity to become animated.

So I started greeting people, and playing with the kids, just like I was in church. Aase's girls immediately realized I was available, and a couple of them grabbed on and did not let go of my hand for the rest of the night, one on my left, the other on my right. My own daughter Jessica just smiled as she knew the importance of my loving these little girls who had come out of such horrendous circumstances and backgrounds. I was thankful that Jessie understood, and this also seemed to mold Jessica's own walk with Christ, as she too has become a warm, outgoing, and giving person towards people.

The lights dimmed, the curtain opened, the program began, and for the next two hours it was as if we were on Broadway, with singing and dancing that touched the hearts of everyone present. Some of the women could play guitar, and one could play the keyboard, and they all seemed like they could act, and dance, and sing. Mongol tradition says that "music was born in Mongolia" so it didn't matter if you were in prison; music and singing were just part of who you were. And so the women sang and danced to everyone's delight, including their own. Talk of therapy! Probably more good was done that night than anyone will ever know.

At the conclusion, a complete surprise award was given to one of the women who would be released from prison to go to England to study drama. She was overcome with emotion as the audience rose to its feet in an ovation to rejoice with the inmate now set free. And finally the head of the prison was introduced and given a robust round of applause as she came to the stage, for allowing such a night to happen. But the reason she had come to the stage was to make the most honored presentation of the evening… to Aase, for it was Aase and the spirit in her that had birthed this evening. Everyone was smiling as a bouquet of flowers were given to her, and we stood in appreciation and admiration to applaud this wonderful servant of God, so unassuming, and self-effacing, and yet so dynamic!

Aase's kids

CHAPTER 17

The Mongolian Evangelical Alliance & A Seminar

"The apostles and elders came together
to look into this matter."
Acts 15:6

It was through the World Evangelical Fellowship and the diligence of the organization Interdev that the Mongolian Evangelical Alliance came into being. How could we cooperate together to fulfill the Great Commission? The fact that a Mongolian Evangelical Alliance was being established in 1998 shows how quickly things were developing in Mongolia. Not all missionaries were in agreement with the founding of the MEA. Some felt it was too soon. Indeed the Mongol leadership was young and inexperienced, but there is no better way to gain experience than by doing.

When things were ready for the inauguration of the MEA in November of 1998, the meeting that night had a decidedly different flavor than other "meetings" that had taken place over the years, which had been led by foreigners. There were traditional Mongolian instruments played at the meeting that night, the *morin khour,* the hammer dulcimer, and the *chantz,* which is a long-necked instrument of three strings that, interestingly enough, sounds a little like a banjo. There were singers dressed in Mongolian dells who led the worship, and the church in Mongolia took a giant step that night towards becoming more Mongolian.

A simple skit depicting a story from the time of Genghis Khan was used to illustrate what the MEA was all about to the delegates of churches who were deciding if they wanted to be members. Amazingly the story is practically right out of the Bible.

Genghis Khan's mother was named Hoelan, and she gathered her sons together and gave each one of them an arrow and told them to break it. The boys obeyed and naturally had no problem breaking the arrows. Then she gave them all another arrow, and this time told them to put the arrows together in a bundle. Now as the boys tried to break the arrows, the combined arrows could not so easily be broken, and so Hoelan told her sons it must be the same with them. They must stay together and learn to work through difficulties. Obviously this was a great application of the Biblical principle set down in Ecclesiasties 4:12, "Though one may be overpowered by another, two can withstand him, and a threefold cord is not quickly broken." Drawing from their own cultural history to make the point was ingenious. And so the MEA was born, and twenty-two churches signed up as members.

The Alliance was open to everyone who agreed with and signed the doctrinal statement, which was based on the Lausanne Covenant. Though the leadership of the MEA would be completely Mongolian, missionaries would be invited to attend meetings as necessary or desired. It was a bit exclusive, but fortunately this nationalistic aspect was temporary and was something the Mongol church leaders needed to work through themselves. This they did, and by the year 2001, the constitution had been amended, so that non-Mongolian leaders were invited to participate as full members.

But there were also some problems in the Church in the fall of 1998 that needed to be addressed. It was apparent that a sufficient equipping of the young Mongol church leaders to deal with sin was still lacking. As a result there was sin in the Church. Missionaries and Mongol church leaders all agreed. But what could be done? How could this corner be turned?

Satan was on the prowl, roaring and seeking to devour the church. There was only one thing to do. Run to the roar. It's a spiritual principle. The passage in 1 Pet. 5:8 speaks of standing firm in faith and resisting the devil, not running away from him. Lions hunt by ambush, placing their game between old lions and the younger lions. The old lions roar and the game runs away from the roar right into the jaws of the younger stronger lions lying in wait. The key is to run to the roar, not away from it. If there is a problem face it, put all the cards on the table and take a look at what's there.

In the end we decided that a series of seminars over the course of the winter might help bring a greater understanding among the church leaders that a standard of righteousness had to be upheld and could not be compromised. The seminars were scheduled for nine o'clock on Saturday mornings, once a month. The church in Erdenet taught the first seminar and over 170 church leaders and missionaries attended.

The Swedish missionary Magnus Alphonce who had planted the church in Erdenet had somehow mastered the art of asking questions rather than making statements. Instead of showing his disciples how much he knew, he tried to make his church leaders think, and other missionaries and Mongol leaders needed to learn this important lesson. This sounds simple, but it is a lot easier said than done.

There were at least a dozen leaders who came down from the church in Erdenet, which now numbered more than 700 people and had over fifty cell groups! They taught through skits, and their Swedish leader gave an excellent history of some of the trials the church had been through and the lessons they had learned.

All of this set the stage for their worship leader who had fallen and been restored, to give her testimony. And suddenly we were on holy ground and you could have heard a pin drop. It was simply not Mongolian to confess sin as she did that morning, but it was entirely Christian and helped many others to understand that in the final analysis they must be Mongolian Christians, not Christian Mongols. This woman's candidness and the wonderful victory that had come to her and to their church as a result of her confessing her sin, and submitting to discipline, was exactly what the rest of the missionaries and church leaders needed to hear. Everyone left that day with a renewed sense of hope.

This woman was so strong and beautiful that I wondered how she would ever find a husband. But the Lord had just the man picked out for her. He had spent four years in prison as a youth. But just at the end of his term in prison, when he was still in his mid-twenties, he heard of Jesus Christ, received the Lord, and was born again. When he came out, someone from Erdenet who knew the worship leader told this young man that there was a woman in Erdenet the Lord had for him. That's of interest to most young men, so he took the next train to Erdenet to see if this could be true, and so it was.

After they were married, they then went back to his hometown of Darhan and together they planted a church, under the supervision of the leadership in Erdenet. The church grew rapidly to over a hundred, and this young couple grew as well. It was not all easy. Some rough edges needed to be sanded off, but together they worked through their difficulties, as all married couples must do. They are representative of many young Mongol men and women who found each other in Christ and entered the ministry as the Lord built His church in Mongolia.

Other missionaries came and taught in the seminar in the following months, each bringing another piece of the spiritual puzzle to put in place. We all knew how important it was to give a clear picture to the young Mongol church leaders of what was required to lead the church. The leader of the German mission taught one seminar, and a pastor from South Africa another. Altogether, five seminars were held over the winter and for the last seminar, I taught on holiness, and what it really meant, as many people had no idea as to the true meaning of the word , which is, "to separate".

In Moses' first encounter with God at the burning bush in Exodus 3, a voice spoke to him saying, "Moses, take off your sandals, for the ground on which you are standing is 'holy' ground." Now if we were to take a handful of the sand from where Moses was standing, and a handful of the sand from a mile away and analyze them under a microscope, we would not find any difference in the two. So what made the ground on which Moses was standing holy? Because from all of the rest of the desert, God had separated this as the place where he would talk to Moses. It had been consecrated to the purposes of God, set apart from the rest of the desert, and this is what made it holy.

Another illustration is that of a knife used to sacrifice a sheep. If a Levite should rush home in a hurry one day and ask his wife for a knife to be used in the sacrificial ceremony at the Temple, the moment that knife became dedicated to the purposes of God, it was transformed from being common... to "holy". It had now been separated, set apart, made holy by an act of consecration.

Finally in Romans 12:1 we read, "I urge you therefore brethren by the mercies of God to present your bodies, a living sacrifice, *holy*, acceptable to God, which is your reasonable service of worship." There is a second act of commitment to the Lord in this verse that has nothing to do with salvation. When we are saved, we are set apart, "made holy" by God as one of His people. But Romans 12:1 is not talking about salvation, but has everything to do with dedication. Once a person is saved, it is then their choice to become consecrated, as we voluntarily separate ourselves away from the world, and unto God. This is a step *we* take, something *we* do, not something God does. Our salvation does not depend on it, Paul is not talking to unbelievers in Romans 12 but believers. However, once we are saved, we can make this decision to separate ourselves to God, which in turn gives us a power to live the way the Bible teaches that we did not have before. "Salvation is only through the sacrifice of Christ, and consecration is only through the sacrifice of yourself to Christ."[6]

6   Bruce Wilkinson, *Personal Holiness in Times of Temptation*, (Eugene Oregon: Harvest House,1998) p.74

Notice that Paul does not *command* the Roman believers to make this commitment to present themselves in this way to live holy (separated unto the Lord), but rather he *invites* us to do so, he urges us to do so. We do not bring someone else to be sacrificed as Abraham did Isaac; we offer ourselves. The gym where we were holding the seminar was quiet, the young Mongols were thinking hard about the things they were hearing. We had been going through the material for over an hour, and finally it was time to make the decision, "Everyone who would like to present themselves to God as a living sacrifice that is holy, let's get down on our knees and talk to God about this step we are taking."

Everyone in the room got down on the floor, and there we stayed for quite some time as people did much-needed business with God. Tears were shed, what is really important was reckoned, and decisions were made, an act of the free will that God gave to man, creating him in His own image. This day, many Mongol church leaders were freely separating themselves unto God, committing themselves to uphold the standard of righteousness that is written in the Bible.

It was fifteen minutes before we got to our feet again, and there was a freshness in the room that had not been there before. It was wonderful! And as a song was in all of our hearts we started to sing, and the renewed eye contact with one another as we sang, told us that we were all standing on holy ground, and had met with God in the last few minutes.

After the seminar, there was a greater sense of purpose in the leadership of the community that was good to see. Not everything was perfect, but they were now committed to upholding the standard of righteousness that is necessary to preserve the Church. It was the spring of 1999, and not only had we come through another winter together, we rejoiced in the reality of the decisions we had made that would change our lives forever, and further the work of God in opening Mongolia to the message of His Son.

Chapter 18

Zorig & A Day in Parliament

"And you shall stand before governors and kings for my sake."
Mark 13:9

Back in 1990, the Democratic Revolution, as it came to be known, was led by the young man Zorig, whose name literally means courage. At a time when Sukhebaatar Square filled with over 100,000 people calling for the government to step down, Zorig's voice was the one that kept things peaceful. A young intellectual, Zorig had attended university in Russia. Politics and freedom for the Mongolian state were his life and passion.

Things had slowly but steadily improved in Mongolia from that historic time in 1990. There were ups and downs and the usual corruption in various quarters. Then new hope came again after the election of 1996, until the newly elected Parliamentarians figured out how to direct the aid money coming into the country into their own private bank accounts. The streets were filled with potholes, but deluxe four-wheel drive Toyota Land Cruisers and Mercedes and BMWs abounded.

In the midst of the corruption, a notorious casino from the island of Macao near Hong Kong, with strong ties to the Mafia was working feverishly to get legislation passed through the Parliament to allow it to set up business in Mongolia. They had easily bought off most of the members of Parliament who had opposed them, and only one now stood in their way, Zorig, the quiet revolutionary whose mother happened to be a Christian could not be bought off. Along with the minister from Foreign Affairs whom I had first met back in 1990, just after the revolution, Zorig and I had dinner together one night back in 1993. A friend of mine in politics who knew Zorig, was able to arrange the dinner.

Zorig was obviously troubled with the concerns that the government was going through. I felt he could use some perspective to help him see the incredible accomplishments he had already achieved. And so we talked a bit of history, mixed with the current events of the day. I knew he had been exposed to Christianity and so as the meal progressed, I shared the gospel with him. He smiled but seemed to be calculating the political ramifications of a commitment to Christ in his mind. At this time the church only numbered a couple of thousand young people out of the 2.2 million people in the country.

Now five years later in 1998, with the beleaguered government looking for its third Prime Minister in five months, though Zorig was only thirty-six years old, his name rose to the top of the list. It was Friday, October 2, and his name would have been put forward the following Monday. The underworld would have to move fast if they were to prevent his becoming Prime Minister, putting him in a position to completely block their efforts to bring their operations into Mongolia. The hit was crude, obviously done by amateurs who were offered more money than they had ever dreamed about, to do something they would probably have never thought of doing. That very night the killers forced their way into Zorig's apartment, gagged and tied his wife up, and put her in the bathroom. Then they waited for Zorig to come home, and when he stepped through the door, they knifed and hacked him to pieces with a hatchet. It was cold blooded murder.

The next morning as the news of his death was announced, the nation went into shock. Zorig, their beloved leader who had fought so hard to set

them free, and then labored so hard to keep them free, as he alone would not give in to the demands of the underworld, was dead. As Proverbs says, "When the wicked rule, the people mourn." It was an unbelievably tragic blow for Mongolia, for Zorig embodied the heart and soul of the Mongol people, the hopes and dreams of the new nation.

Over the years, I wrote a number of articles which were published in Mongolian newspapers trying to exhort and encourage the people in their struggle to find their way in this strange new world in which they found themselves at the close of the twentieth century. Ironically, with the events of the recent months threatening the stability of the country as they searched for yet another Prime Minister, I had submitted the following article to the nation's largest newspaper on October 1, the day before Zorig was murdered. On Tuesday it was in print, and evidently it struck a chord with the Mongol people, for by eight-thirty that morning, it had been picked up by radio stations around the country and was being read over the airwaves to the nation. Perhaps the feeling was it might help take the edge off the loss of their beloved leader, Zorig.

Which Way Will the Mongols Go?

No one ever said that going a new way would be easy. Perhaps this was a misconception that some people had when they decided to go the way of freedom in 1990. To be someone's slave is easy. They tell you what to do and you do it. You don't have to make any decisions. But to set one's own course is another matter.

Perhaps some Mongols thought that if they would simply change systems of government from socialism to democracy that they would all become rich. But this is not the way it works in reality. Democracy does not make one rich, it simply allows for the opportunity to make money and become rich if that is what a person wants to do. Many people have found something better to live for than money such as family, culture, music, literature, social service, teaching school, or their profession. But still it requires hard work to improve one's standard of living. The difference in the two systems of government is that under socialism you must work for the state, and in a democracy you have the opportunity to work for yourself.

So now the new government in Mongolia is having problems. Is this not to be expected? The men and women in Parliament now are no better than the men and women before them, and they too have made some mistakes. But just because this government has made mistakes, is this a reason to quit? A righteous man falls seven times, and rises again, but a worthless man quits when things are difficult. All governments fail at some point but a good government will pick itself up and carry on with the work it has to do.

Perhaps the members of Parliament are feeling discouraged because of the mistakes they have made. But this is no reason to throw everything away. The Mongol people need to voice their support for this government and stop listening to those who only want to criticize. Anyone can criticize, but who can help to build things up? The members of Parliament are not perfect. Yes some of them only want to line their pockets with money and do not care for the good of the country. These people should be replaced at the next election, but many members of Parliament want to work for the betterment of Mongolia and they need the support of the people.

There are forces at work that would want to bring the Mongolian government down and pull Mongolia back into slavery again. But having lived in Mongolia since 1992, I do not believe that is what the majority of Mongolian people want. Things are difficult in Mongolia today, this is true, but compared to other countries in the world, either coming out of, or still under the rule of dictatorship, Mongolia is in a far better condition. Compared to countries such as Afghanistan, Algeria, Croatia, and many other countries in Africa, the Mongol people have much for which to be thankful.

The Mongol people have done well to keep peace in their country, and for this they should be commended by the international community. The Mongols are a marvelous people as they have demonstrated, in carrying on in the face of such a difficult situation.

Now is the time for the Mongolian people to show their strength and perseverance, and show their support for this present government. People should pay their taxes and recognize the good things the government is trying to do. Mongols are a worthy people who should not quit on themselves. The members of Parliament should recommit themselves to the goals and ideals on which they were elected of turning Mongolia into a prosperous nation where people are free, and there is peace. May God give wisdom and courage to the Mongol people and their leaders.

Zorig's killers were never found. The probe initiated by the next Prime Minister, evidently got too close to finding out who was responsible, and he too was replaced.

It was a year later in the last week of November in 1999, that we watched a video someone had sent us called *Amistad*, telling the story of what the movie called the last battle of the American revolution, which brought to a head the issues leading to the Civil War. It was a Monday night and I sat enthralled at the closing scene where former President John Quincy Adams argued the case for the abolition of slavery before the Supreme Court of the United States. The actor's speech was eloquent, moving, and I wanted to speak like that. The opportunity came soon enough.

The next day there was a knock at the door and a courier from the Mongolian Parliament had an invitation in his hand for me to attend a subcommittee meeting that Thursday. I took the invitation and thanked the courier and somehow knew that I would be speaking at that meeting, just what yet, I didn't know.

But the following day the executive director of the Mongolian Evangelical Alliance, Arinbold, knocked on my door. He had in his hand a bill being proposed by the Ministry of Justice, which would greatly infringe upon the freedom of religion of all persons in Mongolia. I listened to Arinbold as he went over the key points of the bill, and I knew as he spoke, what it was that the Lord wanted me to say the following day at the subcommittee meeting. I asked Arinbold if he was free the next day and would he like to accompany me to the Parliament building? I shared that there was to be a meeting and that he was welcome to join me if he liked. Like most Mongols, Arinbold had never been inside the rather august looking Parliament building in the middle of the city, though we all had walked around it many times, and naturally Arinbold said he would be glad to come with me.

I watched the movie *Amistad* again that night as I was sure that was the tack the Lord wanted me to take in speaking to the government the next day. And of course with Arinbold and other Mongol church leaders there, they would be receiving a lesson they would be remembering, so it was important that the right model be presented, which to my mind was one of respect, but not of fear or intimidation. The church leaders needed to know how to stand firm, humbly, but boldly holding the ground regardless of the opposition.

The next day we checked our overcoats in at the ante room and were led into a huge room with long tables placed end to end to make a large rectangle that would seat about seventy. I could see several of my colleagues in the room, many of my very best friends with whom I had served in Mongolia now throughout the decade. And about half of the room was filled with secular NGOs who had a completely different agenda.

At the head table sat the Minister of Justice, his assistants, and a well known member of Parliament and his aids. The Minister of Justice opened the meeting and stated our agenda to review some of the new laws governing NGO activities and then recognized the member of Parliament who read a fifteen-minute speech that had one line in it which looked like it gave me just enough room to speak to the issue of religious freedom that I felt the Lord wanted me to address. Mostly the meeting was about tariffs and customs and when the discussion was opened up, a number of the representatives from the secular NGOs raised their hands to ask questions. And so I waited patiently for the Lord to open up the right time to speak as I knew He wanted me here, and knew what He wanted me to say.

Finally with ten minutes left in the hour, the boring discussion came to a lull, suggesting it would be all right to change the subject, and I raised my hand. The Minister of Justice recognized me, and I stood to my feet. I introduced myself and shared that my organization had been among the first registered in Mongolia back in 1992 when the government started offering registrations for NGOs (non-governmental organizations) and that it had been a privilege to serve in Mongolia during this time of transition. I stated that my organization had started kindergartens in the *ger* districts, and was taking care of street children, and that I had enjoyed working in Mongolia. "However," I said, "it has been extremely disappointing to see the opposition this government has engaged in towards the Christian church in Mongolia." The room got very quiet. No one from the mission community up until this moment had ever openly voiced criticism in a public forum of the government's religious laws or practices. This was a little like the "shot heard around the world".

"The Mongolian people have always been a people who desired freedom of religion in their midst. Even Genghis Khan granted religious freedom to the countries and peoples he conquered. And in this modern era, in 1990, the Mongol people again voiced their desire to be free, but this government has surprisingly sought to restrict the religious freedom

of its people rather than to extend it. So in keeping with tradition and
the religious freedoms guaranteed in the present constitution, I urge
this government to reconsider its attitude and the opposition against the
Christian church in which it has engaged. The government should realize that Christian doctrine teaches believers to support the government,
and that we are here to help the country, just as many of the organizations gathered here are doing, and that this government has nothing to
fear from Christians." And with that I yielded the floor and sat down.

In spite of the fact that my tone was measured and respectful, and
obviously filled with concern and compassion for the Mongolian government and its people, it was the Minister of Justice leading the meeting who turned out to be the author of the bill Arinbold had brought
to me the day before, and therefore the young minister was not at all
interested in listening to what I had to say. He immediately reached for
my organizational registration and suggested I had no business raising
these issues as my organization was registered to do social work and not
religious work. He carried on in something of a tirade for the next few
minutes, scolding and falsely accusing me of activities of which I was
not guilty, and never let me speak again. He slammed his gavel and the
meeting was over.

On the surface it might have looked like defeat, but inside I had
peace like a river, which I can only attribute to God. There was something of a tea afterwards, which the young Minister of Justice did not
attend, but the well known member of Parliament did, and he immediately came over and said he would like to have a word with me. As we
took our tea and moved over to a corner, he said he wanted me to know
that he agreed with me and did not in the least share the sympathies or
the accusations of the Minister of Justice. I told him thank you, and that
I appreciated what he said and reiterated that the Christians' goal is to
serve and that the government had nothing to fear from us. He smiled

and shook my hand and we headed back to the rest of those who had stayed for refreshments.

A number of my colleagues came up to whisper, "Well done" or "Well said," and I think we all knew that it was time we stand firm in our relationship to the government. Our demeanor must always be one of respect. I had not raised my voice, but spoke the truth in love to the best of my ability. Unfortunately the mind of the Minister of Justice was not open, as had been the minds of the men I'd met at the Ministry of Foreign Affairs, nine years before.

The following Monday I was asked to attend a meeting of the Mongolian Evangelical Alliance. It was important that the young Mongols see that they should not try to pick apart the bill written by the Minister of Justice, but to simply oppose it in its entirety as an infringement on religious freedom. In the end they decided that a petition was to be circulated, objecting to the new religious law and urging the Parliament not to pass the law.

During the month of December, several more meetings took place, each one larger than the last, culminating in a meeting attended by more than five hundred people, including the U.S. Ambassador, a strong Christian, and who gave a moving speech, encouraging the Mongolians to stand firm in this hour of testing. Behind the scenes, the U.S. Ambassador was quietly making his own oral petitions to the leaders of Parliament. By now opposition to the new religious law of the Minister of Justice had become a movement with thousands of signatures on the petition. Then as the new year began, and Parliament, not wanting to upset a lot of people who would otherwise support them, saw the handwriting on the wall, and didn't even bother to put the new religious law on the docket for consideration during their upcoming session.

Slowly the Mongolian government came to realize that they had nothing to fear from their people becoming Christians. Instead, they began to understand that Christians make good citizens. They teach their people to obey the law, pay their taxes, work hard, stay informed and be involved in local and national politics, and basically to work toward the good of the whole society.

Furthermore, the government could see that a number of organizations like World Vision, JCS, Help International, and others were doing a lot of good for their country. They were building houses, building schools, taking care of street children, providing disaster relief, teaching English, hosting business seminars, addressing the alcohol problem, and engaging in numerous other social programs that the government was pleased to have them do.

Mongolian Enterprises International Teachers, Missionaries, Street Kid Parents

CHAPTER 19

The Bible

"The grass withers, the flower fades,
but the word of our God stands forever."
Isaiah 40:8

D r. Ralph Winter of the United States Center for World Mission once said that getting the Bible to people in their own language was the single most important task of reaching the unreached peoples of the world. His reasoning was that once people began reading the Bible, their theology would eventually become biblically orthodox. Dr. Winter was not minimizing the need for missionaries going to express the love of God, but was simply drawing attention to the importance of bringing the Bible to people. And so our committee had carried on with its work, checking the manuscripts and submitting them to one another, and to the missionaries who were working with us on the translation.

Boldbaatar was now in the U.S., but the Lord had raised up others to take his place. Our committee had grown to have three Mongolian translators plus another worker to do data entry and reenter corrections as the translators revised and edited the manuscripts. The Lord had brought together four personalities which meshed together in a wonderful way so that the office had a good working environment. It seemed the Lord had once again given us a hedge of protection.

Each member had a slightly different gift to offer. A young woman named Oyuka was our lead translator. She had won the English Language Institute's Summer Olympic contest a few years back and was awarded with a year's free education at a Christian college in the U.S.. I had first met Oyuka back in 1991, when she could hardly speak a word of English, so it was wonderful to see what the Lord had done in her life and that she now felt the Lord calling her to become a full time translator.

Enkamgalan had been discipled by my friend Mike McKay out in Choibalsan and had moved to Ulaanbaatar when he got married. Mike let me know Enkhy was coming from Choibalsan and that he might fit in well as a translator. As I interviewed him, Enkhy seemed to have the right kind of quiet spirit that would stay with the work. He also turned out to have a gift and love for translation. His Mongolian was the best of our team, and often the rest of the committee would defer to his judgment of how a passage might best be worded.

Chimgee was our third translator and she had often translated for me as I taught in her church or at the evangelical Bible school that had been started, where she had studied and then worked. Chimgee had a good understanding of the Scriptures, and the others often commented on the relevance and accuracy of the corrections she would suggest. It was surely of God how the three of them worked together so well, submitting their work to one another for correcting, and finally all agreeing on the changes that needed to be made. To open Mongolia up, God wanted his word available for the Mongol people to read. In the end, all three of them checked the entire text of the Bible, as did three missionaries who were working in conjunction with our committee.

Once again the Korean woman Sara Lee made a major contribution. In the New Testament she had translated 1, 2, and 3 John, but now over a period of several years, for the complete Bible she had translated the entire book of Psalms! Amazing. Another missionary by the name of

Translators Oyuka, Orianhai, and Enkhamgalen

Stan Kirk who had worked on the New Testament with Boldbaatar came to me one day and said he wanted to translate the book of Leviticus. "Leviticus! Why on earth do you want to translate Leviticus?" I asked. His answer stays with me to this day. "Because with all those offerings and feasts it is one of the hardest books in the Bible to translate and it needs to be done right." The Lord certainly has his people.

In October of 1999, the complete Bible was ready to be proofread. The Summer Institute of Linguistics, SIL, sent a consultant to Mongolia to give the MBTC translation what they call a spot check, by back-translating word for word certain passages into English. After a couple of days, the MBTC translators realized the consultant from SIL was a master translator and they had nothing to fear and much to learn from this man. They gladly yielded themselves to his probing and analyzing of the manuscripts. He was just doing his job, and rather than criticizing, he was actually teaching. As a result it turned out to be a great learning experience for everyone. After checking the manuscripts, the consultant said he was pleased with what he had found with the MBTC work and that it was certainly at a standard whereby we could move on towards publishing. However, with the knowledge that the committee picked up as to how to fine-tune their work, the Mongol translators decided to go through the whole manuscript once again, applying the things they had learned from the consultant. This would put the publication date back another six months, but the committee thought it would be worth the extra effort.

It was hard to believe that in only seven years the entire Bible had been translated. I guess it was something of a miracle. It certainly was a testimony to what can be accomplished through working together as a team. As the word of God says, "that they may be perfected in unity, so that the world may know that You sent Me, and loved them, even as You have loved Me." John 17:23. Clearly the Lord had been with us. With all the flack that working through committees receives today the MBTC

was an expression of, "the body being fitted and held together by what every joint supplies, according to the proper working of each individual part, which causes the growth of the body for the building up of itself in love" (Eph 4:16). And again from Romans 12:4-6 "For just as we have many members in one body and all the members do not have the same function, so we, who are many, are one body in Christ, and individually members one of another. Since we have gifts that differ according to the grace given to us, each of us is to exercise them accordingly."

The order with the printer was for 18,000 Bibles, and 10,000 would be coming in the first shipment. When the Bibles arrived, I called Arinbold of the Mongolian Evangelical Alliance and asked what he thought of holding a ceremony to dedicate the Mongolian Bible to the Lord. Arinbold agreed that this was a good idea, and approached the owners of largest movie auditorium in the country, which holds a thousand people.

The books cleared customs on Tuesday, Arinbold secured the movie theater on Wednesday, and scheduled the dedication for the coming Sunday night, July 23, 2000. In recognition of the year 2000 AD, the

MBTC decided to sell the books at the dedication for 2000 *tugrigs* each. This would be about half of what it cost to print the books, but everyone agreed that all people should have an opportunity to have the Bible, and many in the church were very poor and were living on as little as 15,000 to 20,000 *tugrigs* ($15 - $20) a month. A schoolteacher at this time might make only 35,000-50,000 *tugrigs* a month. Even a college professor might only make 60,000 *tugrigs* a month.

Arinbold arranged for a couple of large trucks to bring the Bibles to the theater and by six o'clock in the evening the believers began to gather. The Mongols had come to buy their Bibles! The Bibles were sold before the ceremony so that everyone could have their Bible for the dedication. Arinbold had also invited worship leaders from several churches to come and lead in worship that evening. The auditorium was packed and the spirit was joyful. A ram's horn from Israel known as a *shofar* was blown which brought everybody to their feet with a roar.

The message I chose for that evening was from Jeremiah 29:11-13, "'I know the plans I have for you,' says the Lord, 'to give you a future and a hope.' And the Lord has a plan for each of you. God wants to use you. He wants you to be His coworkers in spreading His gospel around the world. Now let's turn to the New Testament, to 2 Timothy 1:6. Paul tells Timothy to 'fan into flame of the gift of God which is in you,' and you Mongols should stir up the gift that God has given to you. You are a people who have been created to go. Like no other people I have ever met, Mongols have been created 'to go.' You are evangelists. It is the gift that God has given to you as a people. This is your gift and you must use it. You must get equipped and exercise the gift that God has given to you."

The Mongolian Evangelical Alliance presented a gift to the committee on behalf of the Body of Christ for the work the committee had done. It was a large picture of trees and a stream, indicating 'living water,' and a heartfelt word of thanks. The members of the committee were seated on the stage, and now came forward to put their hands on the Bible and together with the one thousand people gathered there that night prayed and dedicated this Mongolian Bible to the Lord. It was a beautiful time to rejoice in God for what he was doing in Mongolia. More than 2400 Bibles were sold that evening.

But that was just the beginning. The next night, I called Arinbold and asked how the sale of the Bibles was going? He said, "The Bibles are all gone."

"What do you mean the Bibles are all gone?" I asked.

"They are all gone," he repeated, "Sold. All of them."

"In one day?" I questioned incredulously.

Mongols don't like to repeat themselves and having already told me twice Arinbold bid me good night with the Mongolian customary closing of a day, "Have a good sleep," and hung up.

Sleep? How could I sleep? I couldn't sleep if I tried.

The next morning I got up early and drove to the container where the Bibles had been stored. I unlocked it, opened it up, and . . . it was empty! Nothing. I might as well have been Peter looking into the tomb of Jesus. *Baaxhweh.* Nothing.

That afternoon I caught up with Arinbold, and there he presented me with all of the money from the sale of the Bibles the day before, right down to the last *tugrig*, and the names of all the people and churches who had bought the Bibles. They had all been sold.

Ten thousand Bibles had been sold in one day! Glory to God!

Not many people knew we were leaving. I didn't announce it at the dedication like I probably should have. I felt our work was done and the

Lord was leading us on, so rather than draw a lot of attention to ourselves, we decided to just slip away. The people at the homeschool co-op we had helped start gave us a going away reception and it was good to be with close friends. We stayed our last night in Aase's flat, as we had sold or given all of our furniture away.

The last week had been hectic, not at all like we wanted. But we squeezed in what we could and were invited to several people's homes for farewells. An old grandmother whom we had brought to the Lord out in Dambadarja had us over to her house. Do you remember the moment when you were saved, the beauty, the wonder, the cleansing, the awe, and the peace? Since her conversion she had brought many of her family to know the Lord and her daughter was a faithful worker in our kindergarten. The grandmother was old and crippled but she loved the Lord, and loved going to church. She had been part of our first home group in Dambadarja, and then a faithful member at Muheen Xair for the last six years. New Life! It is amazing what it does when people receive it.

Packing was emotionally difficult and a much bigger job than we'd realized. But we had to go. Laura was tired and so was I. It seemed like we could see a picture of ourselves in the Song of Solomon 8:5, "Who is this coming up from the wilderness, leaning on her beloved?" To us, that was the way it should be when one comes off the field. Spent. The Lord had given his all for us and we should do the same. The beautiful thing from this verse is that Jesus, our beloved comes out to meet us. He's not some far off God, but one who is with us, and knows what we have been through, one whom we can lean on. He was there.

I gave our van to the Mongolian Evangelical Alliance and we sold or gave away the rest of our furniture and belongings. We took the pictures and mementos that were dear, but neither Laura nor I much treasure "things," so we didn't pack a lot of things to bring home. The work was the thing we came for, and now our part was done.

Yet all too soon the day came to leave. We decided to go by train as it was a third of the price of flying from Mongolia to Beijing, and we also had a fondness for the train. A couple of our neighbors pitched in to help us get to the station. It was a small crowd of people of about thirty who gathered at the station to see us off, mostly just our closest friends. Mike McKay had come all the way from Choibalsan to say goodbye. Young Choon was there with his family, and a few of the Mongolian church leaders, MBTC translators, and people from the *ger* community of Dambadarja.

The tears flowed through our smiles as we hugged one another one last time and said goodbye. It was hard to believe after thirteen years of working toward opening Mongolia to the gospel that our part was about to end. We took a picture together and then leaned out the window of the train as it began to pull away, waving, saying goodbye again and again.

We watched Ulaanbaatar pass by one last time and then about four miles down the track there was someone standing and waving at the train. It was another one of the missionaries whose son had been close to our boys. They were waving goodbye, and as our eyes met and we smiled at one another, he raised a copy of the new Bible high over his head. To God be the glory in Mongolia.

Epilogue

It is now 2006 and the remarkable movement of God in Mongolia continues to grow in power and might. There are now two hundred and forty-six churches in the Mongolian Evangelical Alliance and over three hundred throughout the country. In June of 2005 the Union Bible Training Center graduated forty-one students from their student body of one hundred and thirty. The MBTC translation of the Bible is in its fourth printing and it is now estimated that there are well over 40,000 Mongols who proclaim Jesus is Lord.

The Mongolian Mission Center (MMC) from the church in Erdenet has planted seventeen churches throughout the country. Their church planting efforts have touched the Buriat people in Russia and their teams have taken the gospel to minority ethnic groups down in China who were totally unreached. Finally, they have sent missionaries to long-lost Mongol relatives known as the Hazara people in Afghanistan. Amazing.

The work of the Norwegian woman, Aase, continues to see the Lord's blessing as she reaches out and ministers to hundreds of the poorest of the poor as well as working with the women in prison, and taking care of street children. She is now seventy-four. In March of 2006 she writes, "To see progress is of great encouragement to all of us. We see that our time, effort and funds are not wasted. We invest in the future of Mongolia. Not in stocks and shares, but in people and their lives."

When I look back on all that happened the Lord has reminded me of a word he gave to me as I was on a plane in New Mexico headed for California back in 1990 to talk to the JESUS film people about dubbing the film into Mongolian. I was in my seat reading my Bible when Luke 5:5-7 spoke deeply into my spirit that this was what was going to happen. "When they let down their nets, they caught such a large number of fish that their nets began to break. So they signaled their partners in the other boat to come and help them, and they came and filled both boats so full that they began to sink." Clearly this is what happened and is happening in Mongolia and it is the Lord's doing.

I think back to Mongolia and I am so grateful for my time there. To all of you who knew me as Rick Ax (older brother Rick) my heart is yours, and we are one in our Lord Jesus Christ. I will always remember you. No doubt in the years to come the Mongol believers will themselves write more of this story as it continues to unfold. For as the prophet said many years ago, "Of the increase of God's kingdom there will be no end."

Bibliography

Becker, Jasper. *Lost Country: Mongolia Revealed*. London: Hodder & Stoughton, 1995.

Broomhall, A.J. The Shaping of Modern China. Pasadena, CA: William Carey Library, 2006.

Cleaves, Francis. *The Secret History of the Mongols*. Cambridge, MA: Harvard-Yenching Institute Publications, 1982.

Colson, Charles. The Body. Nashville, TN: W Pub Group, 1992.

DeWitt, David. *The Mature Man*. Sisters, OR: Questar (Multnomah) Publishers, 1994.

Horworth, H.H. *History of the Mongols: 9th-19th Centuries*. London: Burt and Franklin, 1876.

Kemp, Hugh. *Steppe by Step: Mongolia's Christians—from ancient roots to vibrant young church*. Crowborough: Monarch Books, 2000.

Ladd, George Eldon. *The Gospel of the Kingdom*. Grand Rapids, MI: Eerdmans, 1959.

Latourette, Kenneth S. *A History of Christianity*. New York, NY: Harper Collins, 1975.

Montagu, Ivor. *Land of Blue Sky: A Portrait of Modern Mongolia*. London: D Dobson, 1956.

Olson, Bruce. *Bruchko*. Lake Mary, FL: Charisma House, 1977.

Otis Jr., George. *The Last of the Giants*. Grand Rapids, MI: Chosen Books, 1991.

Peretti, Frank. *This Present Darkness*. Wheaton, IL:Crossway Books, 1994.

Piper, John. *Desiring God: Meditations of a Christian Hedonist*. Sisters, OR: Multnomah Publishers, 1987.

Rhys, E. *Marco Polo: The Travels of Marco Polo*. London: J.M. Dent & Sons Ltd, 1908.

Richardson, Don. *Eternity in Their Hearts*. Ventura, CA: Regal Books, 2006

———. *Peace Child*. Ventura, CA: Regal Books, 2005

Wilkinson, Bruce. *Personal Holiness in Times of Temptation*. Eugene, OR: Harvest House Publishers, 1999.

About the Author

Rick Leatherwood was born Sept. 6, 1948 in Ft. Worth, Texas. He was born again June 16, 1979, while homesteading near Anahim Lake, British Columbia. He graduated from Living Faith Bible College in Caroline, Alberta, then studied at the U.S. Center for World Mission in Pasadena, California. He and his wife Laura were married in 1982, and founded Mongolian Enterprises Int'l in 1987. The Leatherwoods now live near ancient Nineva.

Lord Jesus forgive me of my many sins.
Please guide me Lord Jesus through thick and through thin.
For I found I'm unable of running the show.
I wound up lost with nowhere to go.

My daddy said, "Son you're not humble enough.
You're too dog'on proud of being so rough and tough."
But I wouldn't listen or admit that to him,
until I was living in the middle of sin.

There I was with no place to hide.
I felt so ashamed like I surely would die.
I didn't like what I saw when I looked inside,
there was nothing to do, so I sat down and cried.

It's hard to believe that a sinner like me is who Jesus Christ
would love tenderly, but when I cried out in Lord Jesus name,
His love and compassion, and salvation came.

I felt a great load lifted off of my back
and by the sweet grace of God I'm again on the track.
And I pray that I'll stay here the rest of my life
and spend my time loving the Lord Jesus Christ.

July 1979

Rick Leatherwood can be contacted at kairos.rick@gmail.com